GHOST WALKS IN AND AROUND EYAM

NINE WALKS THAT REVEAL THE SPECTRAL SECRETS OF EYAM AND THE SURROUNDING AREA

JILL ARMITAGE

COUNTRY BOOKS

Published by Country Books/Ashridge Press
Courtyard Cottage, Little Longstone, Bakewell, Derbyshire DE45 1NN
Tel: 01629 640670
e-mail: dickrichardson@country-books.co.uk

ISBN 978-1-906789-27-5

© 2010 Jill Armitage

The rights of Jill Armitage as author of this work has
been asserted by her in accordance with the
Copyright, Designs and Patents Act 1993.

All rights reserved. No part of this publication may be reproduced,
stored in a retrieval system, or transmitted, in any way or form, or by
any means, electronic, mechanical, photocopying, or otherwise,
without the prior permission of the author and publisher.

British Library Cataloguing in Publication Data.
A catalogue record for this book is available from the British Library.

By the same author

IN THE PARANORMAL GENRE:
HAUNTED PLACES OF DERBYSHIRE
GHOST PETS & SPIRIT ANIMALS
THE HAUNTS OF ROBIN HOOD
ROMANTIC HAUNTS OF DERBYSHIRE
HAUNTED DERBYSHIRE
HAUNTED PEAK DISTRICT
GHOST WALKS IN & AROUND BAKEWELL
GHOST WALKS IN & AROUND CHESTERFIELD

WALKING BOOKS:
DISCOVER THE AMBER VALLEY

Printed and bound in England by Cpod Ltd., Trowbridge

Contents

   Introduction   5

   The History of the Plague   6

1. Eyam Village Ghost Walk   13

2. Mompesson's Well   57

3. Eyam to Foolow   62
   A resident ghost – superstitious miners & smoking spirit

4. Bretton & Bretton Clough   76
   The phanton hunt & the Gabriel hounds

5. Highcliffe – Stanage – Abney – Highlow – Leam – Eyam Moor – Wet Withens – Sir William Hill Road – Mompesson's Well – Eyam Churchyard   84
   The phantom & the carter – haunted Highlow Hall – lost love – phantom coach – ghost lights & malevolent spirits

6. Riley Graves – Stoney Middleton – Lydgate Graves   95
   The ghost at the graves – phantom figure of Flora – spectre crossing – strange smells at the hall – red returns

7   Riley Graves – Stoke – Froggatt Bridge – Stoney
    Middleton – Lydgate Graves   108
    the ghost at the graves – phantom figure of flora –
    spectre crossing – haunted hall – highwayman's
    haunts – strange smells at the hall – red returns

8   Lydgate – Stoney Middleton – Sallet Hole Mine –
    Black Harry Gate – Eyam Dale   116
    ghostly mines – haunt of the highwaymen – ghostly
    old woman & a phantom cyclist

9   Calver – Froggatt Edge – Curbar   126
    protective dogs – the pretend corpse – phantom
    footsteps – little people & the pumping engine

INTRODUCTION

Eyam (pronounced Eem) is a secluded Peak District village hemmed in by green slopes and majestic hills. Within ¼ mile, the busy world passes by along the A623, yet every year thousands of people head directly to this isolated rural community, tragically famous as the Plague Village.

The year 1665 saw outbreaks of Bubonic Plague in London and many other cities, towns and villages across England. When it arrived in Eyam, in order to contain the disease the villagers chose to lock themselves in isolation and suffer alone during one of the greatest catastrophes ever to befall England; the incomprehensible terror of the plague, caused by the bite of a rat flea infected by the bacterium Pasteurella pestis. This was an act of true altruism by grief stricken people in a village where every home became a morgue and every resident a mourner. With that kind of sad legacy its not surprising to find that Eyam has many poignant ghost stories, but occasionally I found a curiously droll one too.

While out in his Eyam garden one day Dave saw a rat – the fundamental carrier of the 1665 plague virus. No sooner had the fact registered than the rat suddenly raced off across the garden at top speed to disappear under the fence. As he stared in amazement, Dave realised that a misty ball about 30cm long and 20cm high was in hot pursuit. The mist hit the fence, shuddered and broke up. It was a bright summer afternoon yet the mist was perfectly clear and Dave could only conclude that this was a phantom cat chasing its sworn enemy the rat.

Ghost Walks in and around Eyam weaves the plague story into the areas folk history, uncovers some curious facts and fantastically spooky ghost stories. It's a book for enjoyment and recreation, ideal for the armchair walker and those who are fond of a relaxed approach to walking. All the walks begin and end in Eyam, although some can be shortened if alternative start and finish points are preferred, so why not come with us and discover the story of the plague and the ghostly legacy it has left behind.

The village walk is perfect for an afternoon stroll, an evening amble or for extra atmosphere wait until its really dark – if you dare!

If you have encountered any form of apparition, or you have your own ghostly tale to relate, I would love to receive details c/o my publisher, and perhaps feature your story in a future book.

Jill Armitage 2010

A History of Eyam Plague

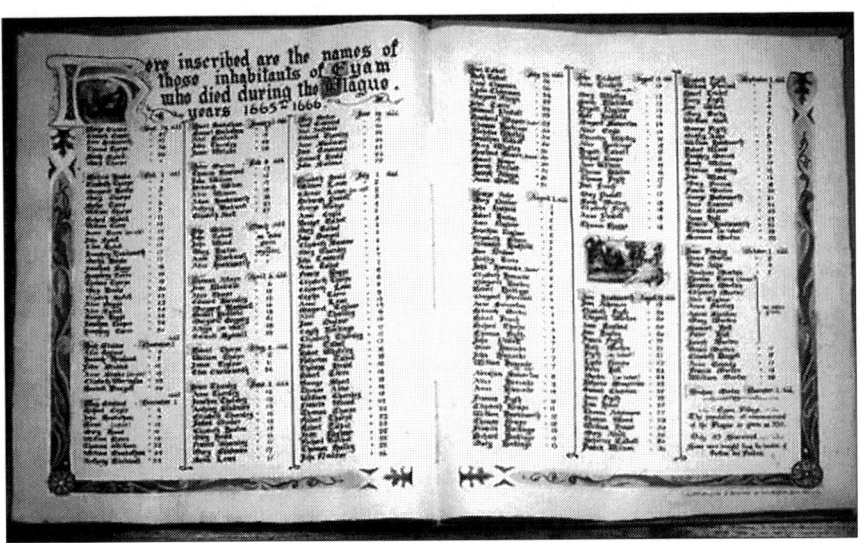

The illuminated list of Plague victims in Eyam Church

Our story must begin between 1642-51 when the whole country was in the grip of the English Civil War. Churches were closed, their contents desecrated. Lead was peeled off the roofs, melted down and made into cannon balls and fighting implements. Lead coffins suffered the same fate. Marriages were conducted before a Justice of the Peace; disputes erupted over respective prerogatives, families were split and neighbours fought neighbours.

In the peaceful village of Eyam, christened in the Saxon tongue – Eaham meaning a well watered hamlet, the tolerance of the Rev. Shoreland Adams, the rector was tested to the full. His loyalty to the King and support of the Royal cause didn't go unnoticed and in 1644, he was seized, deprived of his living and cast into prison. His successor was the virtuous non-conformist minister the Rev. Thomas Stanley of Duckmanton near Chesterfield who continued in this office until the Restoration in 1660 when the Rev Shoreland Adams was re-instated. The villagers were divided in their support for the two clergy, particularly as Thomas Stanley remained in Eyam acting as Curate, ignoring the sneers and jibes of his bitter enemies until he resigned in 1662.

When Shoreland Adams died in 1664, a young curate named William Mompesson, his wife Catherine and their two young children George and Elizabeth arrived in Eyam. William's family were from Scalby in North Yorkshire, and Catherine was daughter of Randolph Carr of Cocken in the county of Durham.

The villagers welcomed the new curate and his young family and looked forward to a period of calm after such a changing pattern of worship, but that was not to be. The year was 1665. Charles II was king, and London was in the grip of the Bubonic Plague, a dreadful disease that came to England along the trade routes from China. It was spread by the bites of fleas which had previously lived on the bodies of infected black rats.

In August 1665, one hundred and seventy miles away in the tiny Derbyshire village of Eyam, a journeyman[1] tailor named George Vicars received a box of cloth from London. Festering inside the box were fleas. The traditional tale says that George lodged at the home of Mary Cooper, a widow with two small sons Edward aged three, and Jonathan twelve. Recent research has uncovered that in March 1665 approximately five months before the outbreak of the plague, Mary Cooper married a tailor named Alexander Hadfield. George Vicars was his assistant or servant who was given the task of unpacking the cloth. Because it was damp, George spread it out in front of the fire to dry, but the heat revived the fleas that were hibernating in the layers of cloth. Within a few days George was ill and on September 7th 1665 died an agonising death. The second death was three year old Edward who was buried on September 22nd. Four more deaths occurred before the end of September and as more deaths followed, the dreadful facts became clear; Eyam had been struck by the deadly plague.

Wealthy residents and those who had somewhere to go, left in a hurry, but there is no record of how many people actually left the village. The

---

[1] JOURNEYMAN – A person whose apprenticeship was complete and who hired out his services by the day (from French journee) or the week.

more affluent landowners and mine owners could have left, but this was a rural community; it was impossible for the farmers to leave their cattle or the shepherds to leave their sheep. Some of the villagers moved out of the close confines of the village and built temporary shacks and huts in the Delph, in the fields near Riley, along Edgeside and beneath the rocks in Farnsley Lane. If more villagers had shut up their cottages and camped on the hillside the number of deaths would have been reduced dramatically, but that's easy to say with three hundred years of hindsight.

The popular belief is that they were told to stay within the village by the Rev. Mompesson, but the local squire, the more affluent landowners and the mine owners would not be dictated to by a young curate who had only just arrived in the village and had sent his own children to safety in Yorkshire. Most of the villagers would stay because they would never have ventured outside the village throughout their whole lives, so the thought of leaving their familiar surrounding would have been as frightening as the plague. Even if they had relatives or friends outside the area it would be questionable as to whether they would get an affable reception or be able to take refuge there.

These were simple, god fearing folks and with no scientific or medical knowledge they believed that the disease was the wrath of God, visited upon the sinful people, a divine punishment that had to be endured. They looked for ways in which they had angered God and pondered on their sins. Was it because two recusant Catholic priests, arrested at Padley Hall some years before were alleged to have uttered a curse on Eyam after being verbally abused by its residents when passing through the village?

It was recalled how village lads had allowed some cows to enter the church and foul the nave while a Wake service was in progress. Was this enough to invoke God's wrath? Some talked about the meteor which had previously been visible in the sky and was interpreted by superstitious villagers as an omen of disaster.

Others remembered that they had heard the sound of the Gabriel Hounds or gabble ratchets as they hovered over the moor above the village. The belief in the appearance of the Gabriel Hounds was very strong in the Peak District and was supposed to be a sure sign that death would soon visit the neighbourhood (see *Walk 3*). White crickets had been seen on domestic hearths, and the more the villagers thought about it, the more obscure omens were remembered, analysed and accepted as clear indications of doom.

Setting aside their deep doctrinal differences, William Mompesson enlisted the assistance and full co-operation of his predecessor Thomas Stanley. Both men were strong in their faith and became the pillars that propped up the anxious community.

There is no reason to think that life in this truly remote, isolated village didn't continue as it had for generations. The few approaches to the village were by rough, narrow tracks, so the village would have been independent and self-supporting. The lead miners and quarry workers would have continued to work, the shepherds would have tended their sheep and the farmers their cattle. Most households would have had a pig or cow and hens would have been plentiful. This was a rural community; there would have been a bumper fruit crop from orchards and hedgerows. Land at village level was either pasture or yielded oat crops and as it was autumn and they had just had a harvest, the village windmill would be busy grinding the oats to make the flour from which oatcakes were made. Oatcakes, cheese and ale would have been the staple diet of most villagers at this period. There was no way that anyone would starve, in fact a lot of food stuff would go to waste. The eggs, butter and cheeses that would have been sold at market would be unwanted by the neighbouring towns and villages fearing that they were contaminated. Who would want infected milk or chickens?

The villagers of Eyam fell into an uneasy routine. They took every precaution to prevent the plague spreading, and the Rev. Mompesson dictated his letters to a scribe outside the village for fear that the paper might contain plague germs. The Earl of Devonshire of Chatsworth House arranged for necessary supplies to be left at specific points on the fringe of the village, the best known being Mompesson's Well on the north road and the Boundary stone between Eyam and Stoney Middleton. Other townships took stringent measures to intercept possible refugees and until recently a record survived at Sheffield concerning *'charges about keeping people from Fulwood*

How could mothers explain to their children?

Spring at the time of the plague at Eyam'.

There were six deaths in September and twenty three in October but the cold days of November which heralded the arrival of a harsh winter were expected to bring an end to the disease. The winter of 1665/6 was said to have been extremely severe and it is not difficult to image the village lying silently shrouded in snow. The cottage eaves would be fringed with icicles hanging like daggers, and the walls would be plastered with driven snow. Deep drifts would have made the lanes inaccessible, completely sealing off the village from the outside world. Inside the damp, dark, stone walls of these cottages, the noxious earth or stone floors would have been strewn with rushes, leaves and herbs with strong disinfectant qualities like rue and bay leaves, believed to keep the plague 'at bay'. They may have camouflaged the problem but in an age of poor hygiene these moist humid conditions provided a perfect breeding ground with plenty of cover and no shortage of food for the many uninvited, unsavoury creatures including the rats that carried the plague. They would also nest in the thatch and rafters of roofs, providing food for the fleas which in turn would ensure the survival of the plague bacillus.

Despite administering medicine to keep the Plague at bay, the noxious floors strwen with rushes and herbs would have provided the perfect breeding ground for many uninvited creatures, as shown in this old woodcut

The winter mortality was less but still above the average, and by the end of April there had been seventy three deaths. In May there were only four deaths and two of those were from other causes, so the villagers had good reason to think the worst was over. They had to have a period of twenty one days free from the infection before being sure, but sadly their hopes were short lived.

Death became so common that the two clergy made the decision that there would be no more organised churchyard burials and internment would take place without passing-bell or funeral rite. The church and churchyard were closed, and the dead were buried in shallow graves in makeshift cemeteries all around the village. The rapidly dwindling population had no heart for anything but marking the graves with wooden crosses or stones to identify where their dear ones lay.

The church was locked and the Reverend William Mompesson, strong in his faith, preached God's word to his slowly diminishing congregation from a rock in the picturesque ravine once familiar as 'Cussy Dell', later Cucklet Church and now The Delph.

The despairing population became listless. The labourer seldom went into the fields, the lead-getter stayed out of the mine, and the shoe maker put aside his leather apron, hammer and last. Gardens and farmland became neglected and overgrown, and rabbits bred until the hillsides were almost over-run.

'The conditions of this place!' wrote the rector in one of his letters. 'My ears never heard such doleful lamentations, my nose never smelt such horrid smells, and my eyes never beheld such ghastly spectacles, the heart breaking sights, the tears, the silent grief, the hysterical woe!'

Not only did William and Catherine Mompesson and Thomas Stanley give comfort and administer to the spiritual needs of the people, they also performed the part of lawyer in the making of wills and numerous other matters. Thomas's brother John, whose name occurs so often in documents during this time was a Chesterfield attorney, but the handwriting and signatures of the Mompessons and Thomas Stanley are attached to many important deeds of conveyance.

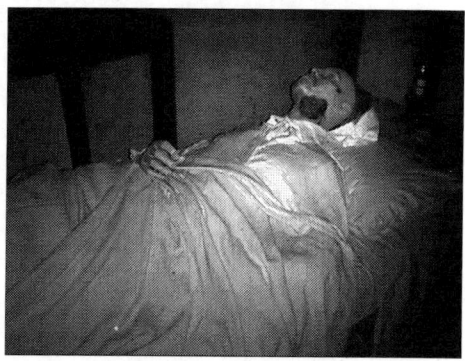

Plague victims died agonising deaths

Catherine Mompesson died on August 25th, exactly a year after the cloth had arrived in Eyam, then in November 1666, after a very long 15 months it was all over but 260 residents of Eyam were dead. Slowly relatives and friends returned to the village to find no smoke ascending from the ivy-adorned chimneys, and a noiseless gloom pervading the lonely street.

But yet no Sabbath sound
came from the village; no rejoicing bells
were heard, no groups of strolling youths were found,
nor loitering lovers on the distant fells.
No laugh, no shout of infancy, which tells
where radiant health and happiness repair
But silence, such as with the lifeless dwells
fell on his shuddering heart and fixed him there
Frozen with dreams of death and bodings of despair.
(WILLIAM & MARY HOWITT)

The Plague window in Eyam Church
Given in 1985 by Mrs C M Creswick. Designed and executed by Alfred Fisher

1: Eyam Village Ghost Walk

EYAM SK215.768: Outdoor Leisure White Peak Area

Eyam

To reach Eyam, visitors from Manchester, Stockport, Macclesfield, Buxton and Glossop, should head for Chapel-en-le-Frith then take the A623. Visitors from Sheffield, Rotherham, Chesterfield and the M1 motorway junction 29, head for Baslow then take the A623. Visitors from Derby take the A6 north to Bakewell, Baslow, then the A623. Eyam is sign posted off the A623. Quarter of a mile up the B6521 takes you into the village centre. Car parking is sign posted, so take the left fork on entering the village and proceed along the main road known as Church Street, passing the church and Eyam Hall on your right. There is a car park off to your left but continue along the main street, pass the post office on your right and after a few yards, turn right by the corner shop into Hawkhill Road. The pay and display car-park is on your right.

Opposite the car park is Eyam Museum outlining the history of Eyam, particularly the chilling facts regarding the plague and its symptoms. Note the weather vane on the roof with the black rat; a millennium gift from the Village Society. A visit to Eyam Museum is highly recommended before or after your walk but as it is seasonal opening only, check times – Eyam Museum 01433 631371; Eyam Village Society 01433 631503.

Our Eyam Village Ghost Walk begins at the eastern end of the village known as Town End and ends at the Museum on Hawkhill Road. To explore the western end of the village known as Town Head, join a shortened version of *Walk 3*.

The Eyam Village Ghost Walk is suitable for everyone to participate in. Because it is mainly on pavements over relatively flat ground, it is suitable for wheel-chair/buggy users. It's ideal for an afternoon or evening stroll or even a midnight adventure, but it is not circular. To make it circular it can be combined with *Walk 2* – Mompesson's well. The combined walk would then start and end at the village car park on Hawkhill Road, starting with *Walk 2* then following the Village Ghost Walk from The Square at Town End.

* Information from the plague is in italics, ghost stories are in boxes.

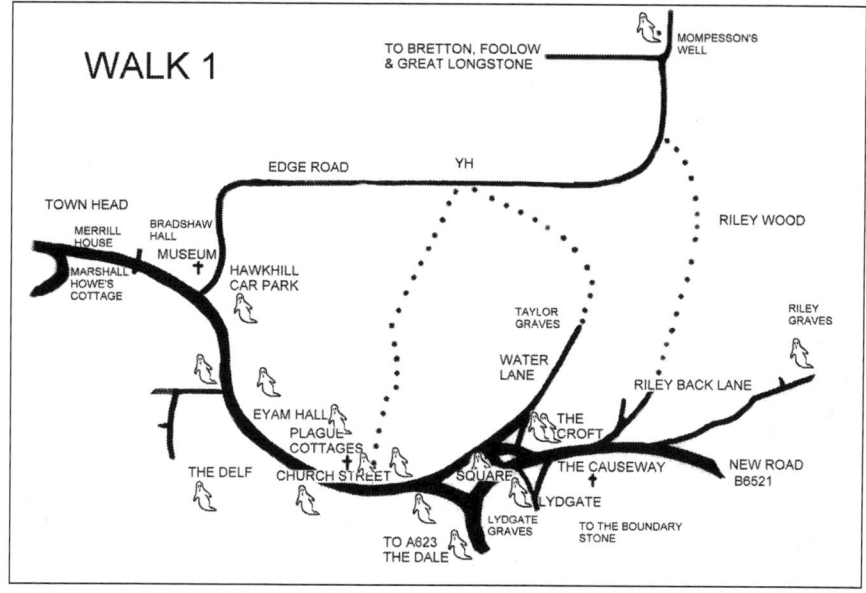

THE SQUARE

As a village, Eyam has developed slowly, gaining a unique character and independence. When necessity arose or circumstances permitted, the occupants simply changed or added to their cottages unfettered by restrictions imposed by rural authorities. A few of the unsanitary cottages have been swept away by clearance orders but fortunately Eyam has many that have retained their period character and their ghosts.

> About thirty years ago, a Mrs Ollerenshaw lived in a cottage bordering The Square and according to the late Clarence Daniel, she regularly saw the former occupant of her cottage; the spectre of an elderly lady in a black dress and snowy white apron, the edge of which she held to her eyes as though to wipe away a furtive tear during some moment of emotional distress.
>
> Another ghostly tale from Mrs Ollerenshaw concerned her grandfather clock that she never allowed to run down. If she did, it always stopped at 9.30, the time at which her husband had died.
>
> Other people have also experienced clocks stopping or chiming at irregular times as if subject to some kind of spirit control. One evening a family sat playing a game of cards, and were surprised when their reliable

> clock chimed twelve at exactly 8.30. They took note of its subsequent chiming pattern but there were no more irregularities. A short time later, they were informed that a close relative had died at exactly 8.30 that evening.

Here in The Square the cruel amusement of Bull Baiting took place until it was banned in the late 18th century. However Derbyshire defied the ban until, according to the Nottingham Review of 9th August 1811, the vicar of Bonsal made a firm stand. He took the Bonsal bullring to which the bull was tethered while being baited by vicious dogs, from the town and deposited it in the church where it can still be seen. Slowly the cruel sport disappeared and the old bull rings were removed, but Eyam, like its Foolow neighbour kept its bull ring, two of the four (another is at Snitterton near Matlock) still in existence in Derbyshire.

This useless reminder of such a barbarous sport lay buried for about 40 years until it was excavated in 1911, then concealed beneath an iron inspection cover. According to Clarence Daniel (1911-1987) the Eyam antiquarian writing in *Derbyshire Countryside* October 1958 – with repeated layers of road-repair material, the level of the road had been gradually raised and the edges and hinges of the cover were sealed with a crust of tarmacadam. By this time, it had become a thing of historical interest, so to make it accessible to the public, the bull ring was raised to road level and the key necessary to raise the lid was placed in the custody of Mr J. M Rylands, a veterinary surgeon who lived opposite the ring in The Forester's House, one of the former seven inns in the village and known then as The Foresters Arms. When improvement work was undertaken in 1986, the ring attached to a heavy chunk of stone was lifted and moved to its present site outside the Peak Pantry Tea Shop on the northern side of The Square.

The Eyam bull ring is outside Peak Pantry Tea Shop in the Square

Throughout our village ghost walk we will encounter the former homes of plague victims and the Peak Pantry Tea Shop is the first. This building is also known as Torre House because John Torre died here on July 29th 1666. His son Godfrey aged eight months died August 3rd 1666, but his wife Joan survived the plague.

Before moving round The Square in a clockwise direction, turn to your left along Water Lane underneath which is a stream. Although there is no river running through Eyam, ironically it is water that gives Eyam its name. Ey is a Saxon word for water and Ham means a settlement. Throughout the village there are many water troughs forming a system that was established in 1558. It is said to be one of the first public water supplies in the country and provided water for domestic as well as agricultural purposes for over 360 years. Clarence Daniel remembered how as a boy it was one of his jobs to make regular trips to the tap in The Square for drinking (hard) water, and a trough opposite which supplied 'soft' water for washing purposes.

In the past, the seven village inns could testify to the fact that Eyam's soft, clear water made excellent ale, and the oldest of the surviving inns is the Miner's Arms on your right.

The Miner's Arms was built during the early 17th century, about twenty years before the deadly plague struck the village. It has been described as a character building with atmosphere and has been labelled the most haunted building in Eyam. That's no mean acclaim in a village where almost every cottage has a resident ghost.

When living at the Miner's Arms, Mr and Mrs A.I. Hall stated that they had heard footsteps walking along the bedroom corridor, and the sound was always accompanied by the rustle of a woman's skirts. The Hall's fourteen year old daughter Wendy was terrified when she felt an unseen intruder in her bedroom leaning over her bed.

When Mr and Mrs Peter Cooke took over the licence, they'd only spent two nights

The Miners Arms claims to be the most haunted place in Eyam

on the premises when, due to a power failure they had to retire to bed by candlelight. As they lay in bed they could hear loud, firm footsteps on the corridor outside their bedroom, but knew this was no human intruder because the footsteps were on floor-boarding, not deadened by the soft pile of the carpet. When the door handle began to move and they felt a definite presence, the landlord searched the room with a candle but found nothing.

That bedroom landing was always persistently cold, even when extra heating was used to try to warm the air, and the bulb in the light socket at the end of the landing fused on a regular basis for no obvious reason. Even more strange was the fact that whenever the footsteps were heard, next morning the door of a cupboard off the landing was always found open. This occurred so regularly even after it had been carefully secured that in the end, they covered it with hardboard and papered it over.

On another occasion, Mr Cooke woke in the small hours of the morning to hear a phantom clock being wound by spirit hands. His daughter's record player would begin to play when no one was in the room and while with a companion, Peter distinctly heard his name being called. The companion verified this.

After the Miners Arms underwent a complete re-vamp, Mr J. A Carnall, chairman of Eyam Parish Council, reported having seen an elderly lady wearing elastic-sided boots, a black bonnet and a cape trimmed with jet sequins enter the back door of the inn. Both the lady and her attire belonged to an earlier generation and according to Mr Carnall, she appeared to be confused and bewildered by the structural alterations. Probably not half as confused and bewildered as Mr Carnall when the lady evaporated before his eyes.

According to local legend, this lady is the 17th century wife of former landlord who died after falling or being thrown down the stairs. Is it her who wanders along that upstairs corridor? Are the heavy footsteps that defy the softening effect of the carpet those of her murdering husband, and did he try to hide her body in that cupboard where the door mysteriously refused to stay closed?

It's not surprising that the Miner's Arms proved to be very active when investigated by a paranormal group called Strange But True. According to secretary Yvonne Gregory, there is much activity in the passages, and a return visit is planned.

If you continue to walk up Water Lane, in a field on the left below Barkers Piece, are the 1666 graves of two sisters Margaret & Alice Taylor plague victims. These two horizontal gravestones lay unmolested upon this sunny hillside near the long vanished home of the sisters, but in later years the stones have been turfed over.

On Water Lane, you will encounter Silk Cottage, a distant reminder of the almost forgotten silk industry established in factories at Water Lane and Town Head in the mid 18th century.

Returning to The Square, turn left to walk past the back of the Miners Arms, an area known as The Croft.

This unconsecrated plot was just one that was used for internment for many families during the plague. Others were buried in land contiguous to their homes. Unlike in many towns where victims were buried in communal plague pits, there is no evidence of this in Eyam. Corpses may have been uncoffinned and the graves marked only by wooden crosses or rude stones, not made to last. The early gravestones that did exist, would have been removed over the centuries and used for alternative purposes. The rough slabs were useful to pave cottage floors and barns. Many were laid as paths and worn by so many feet that any inscriptions or means of identification are now impossible. Often these stones were sacrilegiously broken up for other purposes, but like the previously mentioned gravestones of the Taylor sisters, several grave stones have survived the wear and tear, violation and vandalism of three and a half centuries and we will track them down along our walks.

In more recent years, The Croft became the site of the amusement caterers with their roundabouts, swing boats and coconut shies transforming the old burial site into the annual fairground held during Wakes week.

As in bygone days, the annual Wake begins with a solemn service to mark the religious aspect, and a service in The Delph to recall the heroism of those who died in the plague. Known as Plague Sunday this now marks the beginning of Eyam's well-dressing week in which the village wells are all

The amusement caterers used The Croft in more recent years

blessed and dressed in a custom so typical of the Peak District of Derbyshire.

In Eyam, this custom was revived in 1951 as a Festival of Britain celebration when old ammunition crates were converted into screens. That first design showed the village church and a tableau depicting Adam and Eve. The masonry of the church was largely supplied by broad beans, while workers armed with flashlights raided village gardens to provide the dearth of flowers to create the garden that sheltered the discreetly painted figures of Adam and Eve. The passing years added to the experiences and inventiveness of the well dressers, and even the children got involved with their own 'pippy shows', a corruption of peep shows. They obtained flat tobacco tins or others of suitable size, lined them with soft clay and created mosaics of mosses, shells, petals, pebbles and other materials. These were often displayed in a cavern just down the Dale, where a boy living in a nearby cottage appeared to have a proprietary claim which justified him charging all the other kids for a peep.

Old tins were used by the children to make pippy shows

When they are erected these spectacular Well Dressings have the luminosity of stained glass windows, the colours glowing in their concentrated splendour, and for a week each floral shrine is the focus of attention for visitors and villagers alike. As the days pass, the clay becomes dehydrated giving the appearance of an old oil painting with its cracked and faded canvas, then on the following Saturday the village becomes a charisma of colour and sound as a procession of decorated floats, festival Queens and marching bands parade through the village streets decorated with fluttering flags and garlands.

The next plague cottage we encounter in The Square is now The Eyam Tea Rooms, built as an addition to the Bold Rodney Inn. (01433 631274). Look for the stone trough and its mounting block catering for travellers on horse back that in those far off days could obtain a night's rest at the Bold Rodney Inn.

During the plague years, this cottage was the home of Thomas and Alice Rowland and their family. Hannah aged 15, died on November 5th

1665. Mary her thirteen year old sister died on December 1st 1665 and Abel their ten year old brother died on January 15th. The father Thomas died here on February 14th 1666, but Alice and one son Francis survived the plague.

Abel's gravestone can be seen in the churchyard against the east wall of the south aisle, placed there after being found in use as a paving slab. Abel Rowland died on January 15th 1666 but the stone is marked 1665. This is not a stone masons error; prior to 1752, New Year's Day fell on March 25th so January 1665 followed December 1665.

The Eyam Tea Rooms where the ghost calls – 'It's only me!'

According to the previous owners, the Eyam Tea Rooms are definitely haunted, so could it be Hannah, Mary, Abel or Thomas? It was early January about three years ago when, as new owners, they were revamping the place. That's when people often experience a lot of spirit activity. There's a theory that ghosts get used to the electrical energy that's round the people that inhabit their building. When those people move out, the energy changes and they are disturbed, confused and disorientated. Once the new owners have settled in and the energy levels are stable again, the spirits can settle again, and this is what we believe happed here at the Eyam Tea Rooms

Drawers would mysteriously open and unexpectedly close, things went missing, and music turned on and off, but possibly the most bizarre thing was that the door would open and close and a voice would shout 'It's only me.' When anyone went to investigate they found no-one there. They mentioned this to the butcher opposite, who said that was exactly what the old man who used to live there used to say when he arrived back.

As a child Clarence Daniel lived in a cottage that had been the village's communal 'mangle house'. Housewives would take their clothes to be mangled on a cumbersome machine operated by a series of wooden rollers. When mangles became available to most householders, the redundant village mangle was dismantled and transferred to the joiners shop across the way where it was converted into a bench. Just another example of how village communities were thrifty and never wasted valuable resources.

> In the cottage next door to the Eyam Tea Rooms lived a sea Admiral who set sail in 1768 with Captain James Cook aboard HMS Endeavour on his famed expedition of the South Seas. Within hours of his departure, the Admiral's cat went missing and when it didn't come home week after week, month after month, the family had to accept the obvious that the cat had died. For three long years the Admiral's family waited for his return then one day in 1771, the cat turned up fit and well and settled down as if he'd never been away. What was even more amazing was that within two hours the Admiral returned from his long sea voyage.

Lydgate

Walk away from the Tea Rooms and on your left at the end of this block is the village post box and telephone, and the entrance to Lydgate. Lyd or Lid is a Saxon word which means to cover or protect. This was the main road out of Eyam to Stoney Middleton before the road was cut through Eyam Dale in the 19th century, and at its entrance was a strong gate at which 'watch and ward' was kept every night between 9 p.m and 6 a.m. Every able bodied, male householder in the village was officially bound to take a turn at this gate to question anyone entering the village. As watchman he had a large wooden halbert or watch-bill for protection, and when he came off duty in the morning, he took the watch-bill and reared it against the door of the next watcher. This custom was practiced into the 18th century with Eyam being one of the last villages to retain this very ancient ritual.

As you walk along Lydgate, on your right is Rose and Fossil Cottage. During the time of the plague, this was the home of John and Francis Wood.

Ironically, two hundred years later it became the home of William Wood (1804 -1865) Eyam historian and village chronicler, unrelated to the previous occupants. William Wood's grandfather moved to Eyam from Wigan in 1717 as a servant of the Rev Edward Finch, and later ran an inn by the side of the church on the land now used for the annual sheep roast.

William Wood has left us a rich legacy of Derbyshire stories and in his *Tales and Traditions of the Peak*, he relates stories about Eyam that happened virtually on his doorstep. His cottage on Lydgate would look down over Eyam Dale, the setting for this popular ghost story about a haunted cottage.

William Wood and Clarence Daniel both did much to promote Eyam

There was once a cottage in Eyam Dale, the site of which is now occupied by a house enlarged from two houses built last century. The cottage was haunted by a ghostly woman who was responsible for stripping the bed clothes off sleeping occupants, then tormenting them by pummelling and pinching their defenceless bodies as they lay trembling and frozen with fear. Strong doors and locks could not hold her back. She was seen to enter like a puther of smoke through the keyhole or small holes in walls.

Perhaps she was reliving those traumatic days of the plague and trying to warn the occupants to leave while they still could. She obviously succeeded because people left on a regular basis and more often than not the cottage was vacant. Eventually it fell into a sad state of disrepair but this didn't stop the ghostly visitations. Described as 'rather more than middle aged, wearing a short bed gown, linsey petticoat, mobbed cap and shoes with shiny buckles' this phantom figure was regularly seen hurrying across Eyam Dale and disappearing into the ruined cottage.

This story was so well known locally that there is a spin off about a drunken lead-miner named Tom Loxley who had an encounter with the spectre after expressing his disbelief and lack of fear of such apparitions.

The Golden Ball Inn that used to stand at the Stoney Middleton side of Eyam Dale was much frequented by the local miners and at the time of this story, it was kept by a man called Stephen and his French born wife Blandino known to everyone as Blandy. She was an agreeable woman, but had perfected the art of mining the miners, plying them with drink for however long they had money in their pockets.

Tom Loxley, known to everyone as Cockeye, was a regular at The Golden Ball Inn and although frequently worse for drink was always in good humour and popular with everyone. It was late one evening when his mates were ready to leave that they began to torment Cockeye, reminding him of the dark journey he faced alone through Eyam Dale past the ruins of the haunted cottage. The locals shunned it by day and avoided it at all cost at night because in this crumbling, ivy-clad hovel they believed there lurked a malevolent ghost who was often seen on moonlit nights flitting across the valley at great speed.

'Come on Tom,' laughed Blandy. 'Take another drink to rally your spirits. Surely you are not afraid of a woman, dead or alive?'

The other miners laughed and Cockeye naturally rose to the bait and declared, 'No, nor the devil himself. Pour me another drink Blandy.'

Stephen, the landlord was not comfortable by such talk. He was firmly of the belief that if you call the devil he will come in his own time. Cockeye set off from The Golden Ball Inn full of confidence and bravado vowing to face any ghost which might lurk in the lonely dale. He was in a jocular mood when he left the warmth and comfort of the lamp-lit room of the inn to make somewhat unsteady progress up the Dale towards his home. As he proceeded along the moonlit way, tree shadows assumed fantastic shapes and the babble of the wayside brook suggested to the drunken miner that he was surrounded by ghostly voices engaged in excited conversation of which he was the subject. Loxley's courage was now rapidly oozing away and he began to regret some of the comments he'd made, especially as he approached the old ruined cottage and imagined the ghostly tenant leaving the shadows and approaching him in angry confrontation. His courage began to ebb and his drunken imagination seemed to see in the shadows a twisted human form that moved and writhed towards him. He stood transfixed, too terrified to go on, too frightened to turn back in case the thing should rise up and pursue him. As his senses began to reel, the poor fellow staggered and with a choking groan his legs gave way and he fell face down in the dirt. Shaking uncontrollably, he felt his ankles gripped by icy hands as he was dragged at a fast pace down the dell. As the grip tightened and the coldness increased, he lost consciousness.

It was warmer, gentler hands which gripped and shook Cockeye

> awake in the morning. Stephen, the pub landlord had found him half in and half out of the stream which winds through the dale. Its icy waters had nearly frozen him to death.
>
> There were some that said that it was all conjured up by Cockeye's drink-sodden mind; that the icy grip of the ghost was the water of the stream he had fallen into, but no one could convince Cockeye of that. He stuck to his story for the rest of his life and never touched another alcoholic drink.

To continue our walk along Lydgate, the next stop is Lydgate Cottage.

By the side of Lydgate Cottage are the 1666 plague graves of Thomas and Mary Darby in a small, walled enclosure which was once part of the Parson's field – a piece of Glebe land now occupied by a small housing estate. These are known as The Lydgate Graves. George Darby died on July 4th 1666 and his daughter Mary aged 20 died on September 4th. Tradition says that Mary Darby was seized by the plague as she gathered flowers for her fathers grave and died the following day, but George's wife survived and died in 1674.

A hundred yards further, on the right of Lydgate is The Rock, the former home of Clarence Daniel, (1911-1987) the Eyam antiquarian and lifelong resident of Eyam whose ancestors survived the plague. Clarence published the first of his books about Eyam when he was twenty one, illustrating it with his own drawings. From early youth he avidly collected everything associated with his native village and in 1976 achieved his dearest ambition of opening a small, private museum at The Rock, to display the treasures which he had accumulated throughout his life. After his death in 1987, his wife Cecily donated his collection to the Eyam Village Society, in the hope, now realised that it would inspire the foundation of a museum.

The Lydgate graves of Thomas and Mary Darby

The Eyam Museum opened in 1994 and is opposite the Hawkhill car park

On *Walk 8 & 9*, we continue along Lydgate to Stoney Middleton, passing the boundary stone where money was left in exchange for goods during the plague year, but in order to continue our village walk, return to The Square and turn left. On your left was once the site of the village Pinfold where stray animals were kept until their owners paid a release fee.

The village street

Leave the square and cross the road leading down to Eyam Dale, unless you want to encounter the phantom figure wearing a short bed gown, linsey petticoat, mobbed cap and shoes with shiny buckles or the phantom cyclist – see *Walk 8*

Walk straight ahead until arriving at the lower entrance to Eyam Dale House.

Eyam Dale House

This small country house which is now a retirement home was recently the executive headquarters of Glebe Mines Ltd which became affiliated to Laporte Industries Ltd in 1959. It was once the home of Thomas Bird, an Eyam antiquary who entertained many important guests at Eyam Dale House including royalty. Prior to this, it was known as Eyam Terrace – owned and occupied by Thomas Fenton who inherited much of the property of his maternal grandfather, Philip Weldon.

Thomas Fenton was a surgeon who is said to have participated in the illegal traffic of 'body snatching', when lonely churchyards were robbed of new tenants to procure bodies for experimental purposes in order to expand the surgeon's knowledge. Religious beliefs and common superstition made it unthinkable to disturb a person's remains and most people firmly believed that redemption required the body to be buried whole which meant that the only human bodies available for examination were those of executed criminals.

The supply was never equal to the demand so many villains turned body snatching into a lucrative business, but it was necessary to take only the naked body. In the eyes of the law, there was no property in a dead body, so it could not be stolen, but if a ring or the shroud was taken with the body, the thieves could be severely punished. In order to avoid this, the body snatchers (resurrectionists) would dig up a body, drag it from the grave, strip it of the shroud and any other possessions, bundle it in a sack and trundle it away. If time permitted, the shroud would be returned to the coffin which would then be covered again to conceal their clandestine activities.

Although the subject is not pleasant, the practice of body snatching has left us with some amusing stories. One night, two rascals arrived on the doorstep of the local surgeon with a body trussed in a sack.

'Take it down the cellar,' the surgeon said, then paid the men who headed speedily back to the local tavern. The doctor went down to examine his purchase and found that the body was not dead, just dead drunk. The following night, 'the body' shared the fee with his pals in yet another drunken spree.

> Could this trade have left an impression in the ether? Is this why sensitives who have walked onto the waste ground below Eyam Dale House car park have felt an atmosphere here? People on previous ghost walks have reported feeling scared for no obvious reason, and psychics have also picked up on the feeling.

Alternatively the feeling could be associated with another dreadful event that happened at Glebe Mine which extended under the whole of this area – the church, school and Church street. The mine was closed in 1884 but was re-opened in 1937 due to increased demand for fluorspar, barytes and lead.

> Many years ago, two young women arrived in Eyam without a penny and without wishing to besmirch their reputations, lived at the camp set up by the lead miners. One day a lamp was overturned causing a fire in the hut which was over the entrance to the mine shaft. This badly burnt one woman and trapped the other. People shouted to tell her to go down the shaft until the fire had stopped, but in her panic she tripped, fell down the shaft and was killed. It is said that sensitive people pick up her terror and torture, and her ghost is heard screeching in agony.

Eyam Dale House is also the setting for another haunting story that first appeared in William Wood's book – *Tales and Traditions of the Peak*. It's about the Weldon family who lived at Eyam Dale House around 1770 when this story takes place.

The village spectre

> Twenty year old Mary Weldon, the eldest of the Weldon's five children went to stay with friends in Lancashire, and while there, she met and fell in love with a young man named Baldwin Laycock. The affection was mutual and on the day before Mary left Lancashire, Baldwin asked her to marry him. Mary accepted and in high spirits Baldwin rode over to Eyam to ask Mary's father for her hand in marriage. The agreement was obviously acceptable and that evening as they waited for Mary to arrive back in Eyam, Baldwin sat with her father in the shade of the sycamore tree in the garden. After some time, they were on the point of retiring to

the house when they were startled by the appearance of a shadowy form. It was the figure of an elegant young woman clothed in a long white dress. She had a striking but deadly and cadaverous expression yet there was a calmness on the silent face and a smile loitered on the colourless lips. Then the figure slowly dissolved leaving Mr Weldon in a state of shocked disbelief.

When this disquieting experience was related to Mrs Weldon, she shared her husbands concern, then when she had recovered her composure, explained to the bewildered visitor that they had seen the village spectre. The ghost hadbeen that of Isabel, the eighteen year old daughter of Squire Bradshaw of Bradshaw Hall. Isabel had been compelled to repudiate the affections of her true love and marry a suitor chosen by her father. About an hour after the forced wedding ceremony, the reluctant bride received news that her despairing lover had taken his own life and a few hours later Isabel also breathed her last. Ever since that day, the spirit of Isabel appeared to forewarn of the death of anyone 'whose heart the tender passion fills' or to put it in modern day parlance, it looked as though the love affair of Baldwin and Mary was about to come to an abrupt end.

An elegant young woman appeared in the garden then slowly dissolved

As Baldwin Laycock and the Weldons waited anxiously, a messenger arrived with the news. The coach in which Mary Weldon was travelling home had been about ten miles from Eyam when it stopped. Mary stepped out, missed the step and fell under the vehicle which passed over her body, causing fatal injuries. The time of the accident coincided with the appearance of the village spectre.

In more recent times, at least one psychic has reported seeing a white lady in this area despite having no previous knowledge that a white lady is said to haunt this spot, so could this beautiful young apparition be Mary Weldon or Isabel Bradshaw?

Return to the road, opposite the Victorian school built in 1877 with stone from the old windmill, (see *Walk 3*) and turn left up Church Street.

The irregular street is fringed with homely cottages and knots of houses devoid of architectural discipline, but dotted amongst them are several dignified buildings making a very pleasing street scene. At one time all the cottages would have been thatched but they've been re-roofed with slate from the now redundant slate-pits near Eyam.

The Rectory

Over on your right is the rectory, said to be haunted by the ghostly whisper of Mrs Catherine Mompesson, the rector's wife who died there on August 25th 1666.

People staying at the rectory report hearing noises in the night as if someone is ill and needing attention. It is not unusual for overnight guests to enquire next morning, who was ill in the night. They hear footsteps rushing along the corridor, doors opening and closing and the rustle of feminine dresses. A former maid at the rectory met a ghostly lady descending the back stairs, and afterwards when describing her, it was believed to be the ghost of Catherine Mompesson.

A maid at the Rectory saw a spectre believed to be Catherine Monpesson descending the stairs

The Rectory has been home to some very interesting people apart from the Reverend Thomas Stanley and Reverend William Mompesson, rectors during the period of the plague. A rather more colourful vicar was the Reverend Joseph Hunt who was appointed the rector of Eyam on March 21st 1684.

The Mock Wedding

Rev Hunt hadn't been in Eyam long when Matthew Fearns, one of his parishioners and landlord of the Miners Arms, asked him to baptise his newborn child. After the ceremony, the congregation and the rector were invited to participate in the custom of 'whetting the baby's head' at the Miners Arms. In the merrymaking that followed, Joseph got a little drunk and began to make advances to the landlords eighteen year old daughter Ann.

Egged on by the drunken revellers, Joseph produced a Book of

Common Prayer and went through the Solemnisation of Holy Matrimony ceremony with Ann. Amid a lot of hilarity, each made the customary vows and promises in a mock wedding ceremony conducted by one of the other guests and witnessed by the whole gathering.

Eyam Church vestry was extended for the use of the Reverend Hunt and his family

News of this didn't take long to reach the Bishop of Derby who was furious and adamant that Joseph should marry Ann in the proper manner, so in order to right the wrongs and confirm the union legally, they were married in church on September 4th 1684. As their first child was born two months later, it would appear that their mock marriage was consummated too.

But this news did not please one particular Derby lady who had been under the impression that once Joseph had settled in his new parish, she would become the new Mrs Hunt. Research has been unable to provide her name but she was undoubtedly affluent and shrewd. She proved in the eyes of the law that she and Joseph had been legally betrothed and brought an action against him for Breach of Promise.

Years passed in litigation which drained Joseph's purse and estranged his friends until eventually, deeply in debt and pursued by bailiffs, he and his family were forced to claim sanctuary in the church. They took up residency in the vestry which apparently was enlarged for their convenience.

In this humble appendage to the church Ann and Joseph spent the remainder of their married life with their nine children born between November 1684 and August 1698.

Ann died in 1703 and Joseph on December 16th 1709, so it seems fitting that having lived and died there, an unobtrusive stone in the corner of the vestry at the end of the North aisle should mark Ann and Joseph's final resting place. But what of the children? Their home was the vestry, their playground the graveyard so is it surprising that evidence of this should have lingered?

On numerous occasions, families attending the graves of their deceased relatives have reported seeing a little girl playing amongst the gravestones. She is so real, that on each occasion she has been mistaken for a visiting child. All the reports verify that she is about eight  years old and dressed in period clothes. She dances and plays and has even interacted with other children, then she simply fades away.

Is it possible that she could be singing the old nursery rhyme – Ring a ring of roses, a pocket full of posies. Atishoo, atishoo, we all fall down.

This children's nursery rhyme is a reminder of the plague. The ring of roses refers to the body rash; the pocket full of posies were the herbs carried in an attempt to ward off the disease. The sneezing was a symptom of the plague, which when caught would lead to falling down – dead.

Eyam Rectors

The living was mainly derived from the parish's lead mines, and with the discovery in 1717 of the rich lead bearing vein that runs along Edgeside to the north of Eyam, the living rocketed from a modest £150 to the incredible sum of £1,600 per year. Such an attractive stipend created competition for the pulpit amongst the titled gentry. First there was the Hon. Dr Edward Finch, 5th son of Sir Heage Finch, Earl of Nottingham, then the Hon Thomas Bruce, second son of the Earl of Kincardine. They were followed by the Rev Thomas Seward who was responsible for extending

The vast Georgian Rectory when the rich lead mines provided a lucrative living for the Eyam clergy

the rectory and building the vast Georgian addition.

It was the Rev. Thomas Seward who on the last Sunday in August 1765, to mark the centenary of the outbreak of the plague, stood where Mompesson had stood in The Delph and preached a sermon as he had done. There was also a service to mark the bicentenary, and the service in its present form has been conducted every year since 1910. The day has become known as Plague Sunday.

Village women in 17th century dress attend the Annual Plague Service

His daughter Anna who became a relatively successful poet, was born at the Vicarage in 1747, but the value of the living was shrinking gradually during this time. According to Anna Seward, writing in 1786 – 'the value of Eyam living to my father, once near £700 per annum is not now more than £150'.

Rev. Thomas Seward's successor, the Rev Charles Hargrave was a speculator. He and several influential neighbours provided the capital for the first steam ship service to operate on the River Mersey at Liverpool. The first vessel to carry passengers was named the Elizabeth in honour of his daughter, but the venture did not prove financially successful. Sadly the poor rector was having even more financial problems as another story taken from William Wood's book *Tales & Traditions of The High Peak* tells us.

The 2009 well dressing at Town End dedicated to Anna Seward – to mark the 200th anniversary of her death

The Churchyard Incident

In the year 1790, the Rev Charles Hargrave became the new vicar of Eyam thanks to the generosity of a worthy aunt who purchased the living for £2.000 from someone referred to rather mysteriously as the Duchess of C. A few years after the purchase, both the aunt and the Duchess of C died, and after a lapse of several months, the rector received an order from the successor of the deceased Duchess, requiring payment of the £2,000. The rector had never for one moment considered that the purchase money was unpaid, and although all his aunt's papers were strictly scrutinized, they could find no proof of the payment. Without this proof, the young Duke of B who had inherited the Duchess of C's estates, pressed for payment.

By this time, the rector and his wife had three young children and the upkeep of a ponderously rambling rectory. The lead mines had closed down so the proceeds of the living were reduced to a comparative trifle and the rector had no means of raising the money. Although his family and friends were all sympathetic, they could not help financially, so the Duke commencing legal proceedings and a warrant was issued for the arrest of the Rev. Charles Hargrave. Unable to pay, he would have been thrown into debtor's prison but each time the law hounds arrived in Eyam, the vicar was immediately taken to a secure hide-out where he stayed concealed until they had left. During the following five years, many attempts were made to arrest the rector but all failed thanks to the vigilance and devotedness of the villagers.

Eventually two Bow Street runners named Digby and Brownlow were sent to Eyam. They had a 100% success rate when it came to apprehending criminals and they had a scheme which they considered would be fool proof. The plan was to enter Eyam at the dead of night and secrete themselves in the churchyard adjoining the rectory and arrest the rector at day break before any of his parishioners were able to alert him. Digby and Brownlow entered the village and

The ghostly figure came towards them

> made their way to the churchyard unseen. After stumbling over graves, they seated themselves under a stunted yew tree and for a few minutes they sat in silence listening to the rustling of the leaves and the low moan of the wind in the swaying branches. It wasn't long before their surroundings began to imprint strange impressions on their minds. The two brave men were not feeling quite so brave when they noticed a figure, the semblance of a woman or ghost, coming towards them. Trembling with fear, they watched as she stopped about ten yards from them and in a strange unearthly voice murmured 'Robert, come forth............ Come Robert. Come forth.'
>
> Up sprang the terrified men, leaping and stumbling over graves. They left the churchyard and the village, watched by the demented old woman who wandered into the graveyard every night in the hope that she could call her long deceased husband Robert back from his grave.
>
> What was written in Digby and Brownlow's report is not known but from then on, the rector was left in peace.

In 1960 a major re-modelling of the rectory was carried out to bring it up to modern standards of comfort and convenience. The builders removed the derelict kitchen premises which had long been sealed off from the rest of the building, and knocked down the imposing three-storied Georgian wing, but the 1960's design incorporates the earlier proportion of the house which had been occupied by the plague heroes, Stanley and Mompesson.

The Chapel of St Helen and the Church of St Lawrence

Next door to the rectory is Eyam Parish Church, now dedicated to Saint Lawrence, a Christian preacher who, when asked by the Prefect of Rome to hand over the treasures of his church, presented his people. Angry at being tricked, the Prefect ordered Lawrence to be put to death by being tied to a grid iron and roasted. St Lawrence's badge is a grid iron.

Eyam Parish Church

The site of the present church has existed as a place of worship since Saxon times yet there is no mention of a church or a priest at Eyam in the 1068 Domesday

Book. The first indication of a building is the chapel of St Helen said to have been founded by the Stafford family of Stafford Hall, and incorporated into the present church as the North Aisle. Hanging in the vestry is a bronze lamp of Tudor origin, which if genuinely connected with the church should hang in the north aisle as it is claimed to be the original lamp of St Helen kept burning on the altar as a condition of tenure whereby the Staffords held properties in the district. (See the later story of The Staffords and their strange tenure). The Staffords pew from that earlier church was made into the screen which now encloses the belfry.

The chair believed to be the one used by the Rev. Mompesson during the Plague, but does he use it still?

In the rectors vestry is a Bronze Age Cinerary Urn discovered on Sir William Hill. Its discovery is described in the 1912 edition of the *Derbyshire Archaeological Journal*, and in the choir vestry is a reproduction of an oil painting of Rev William Mompesson. The original is at Southwell Minster, because after the plague Mompesson left Eyam to take over the living at Eakring a parish in the Southwell district.

A wander round the church is highly recommended as there are some very interesting things to look out for. Thomas Stanley and William Mompesson would have spoken from the Jacobean pulpit. The plague register showing Eyam's death toll during the plague is on display in its glass case, and not to be missed is the magnificent plague window. There's also a brass tablet in memory of Stanley and the two Mompessons.

We are told that after the plague, William Mompesson personally supervised the destruction of all materials calculated to conceal germs. Furniture, clothing and bedding were burnt on huge bonfires, yet there is a popular belief that the cupboard in the North Aisle of the church was made from the plague infested clothes box.

Until recently when it was moved to the museum, the chair believed to be the one used by Mompesson while in Eyam was also in the church. Made of oak and carved with the inscription Mom 1662 Eyam, the panel in the back is carved with a crude representation of the Virgin and Child. It was rescued from a Liverpool antique shop by the Rev Canon E

Hacking, a former rector, and presented to the church. At Cheltenham, a carved settle bearing the names of William and Catherine Mompesson was offered to the village, but was not purchased. A striped glass, formerly displayed in the museum of Poole's cavern, Buxton, was purported to be a personal possession of Mompesson. Adding an extra flourish, it was said to have held vinegar in which coins were washed during the plague, but along with other exhibits, the glass was stolen during a raid.

The Churchyard

Moving out of the church and into the front churchyard you will find the 8th century Celtic Cross, one of the finest of its period. It is rich in quaint carvings, rudely sculptured figures of angels bearing crosses and blowing trumpets, and its sides are curiously adorned with scroll-work and interlacings. The cross was employed in every sacred ritual, designed to excite sentiments of piety or compassion and reverence. Originally placed by the wayside, these crosses had a double meaning. They were where itinerate priests and monks would preach when in the area, and on the high-road the cross was frequently placed to deter highwaymen and restrain other predators in the same way that in the market place, the market cross was a signal for upright intentions and fair dealings. Many of these crosses in public places were removed and destroyed by an Act of Parliament in 1643, but local citizens circumvented the wishes of parliament by concealing these crosses with the intention of re-erecting them when the government policy changed, which it was likely to do at short notice during the Civil War. Others can be found at Bakewell, Hope and Chapel.

> *It's unsure whether any of the early plague victims were buried in the churchyard, but as the numbers increased, we do know that bodies were buried all around the village. Apart from Catherine Mompesson, the headstone of Abel Rowland is the only one that can be found in the graveyard near the sundial, but that is not in its correct position as it was only placed there after it was discovered serving as a flagstone on the floor of one of the cottages. Abel Rowland died on January 15th 1666 but the stone is marked 1665. This is not a stone masons error; prior to 1752, New Year's Day fell on March 25th so January 1665 followed December 1665.*
>
> *The table tomb of Catherine Mompesson who died on August 25th 1666 was designed by her husband with its inscription 'Beware ye know not the hour' in Latin.*

> 'Catherina, vxor Gvlielmi Mompesson hvjvs Ecclesiæ Rect. filia Radvlphi Carr, nvper de Cocken in comitatv Dvnelmensis, armigeri. Sepvlta Vicessimo Qvinto die mensis Avgti, Ano. Dni., 1666 ;'

The words on the grave of Catherine Mompesson

A red wreath is placed on the grave of Catherine Mompesson by the wife of the incumbent of the day, to mark the anniversary of Catherine's death

A visitor to the grave of Catherine Mompesson on Plague Sunday will find a wreath of red flowers upon it. It's a long established custom that the wife of the incumbent of the day, places them there because not only is the last Sunday in August close to the anniversary of the outbreak of plague in 1665, a year later on August 25th Catherine Mompesson was buried.

We know very little of the private life of the Rev. Thomas Stanley, born at Duckmanton, near the Royal Hospital at Calow, Chesterfield. He was married with at least one son named John. His wife died in Eyam on June 14th 1664 and is buried in the churchyard. Stanley remained in the village and died there in 1670, but although he is buried in the churchyard, the location is now unknown. There is a monument to him adjoining the priest's door, a stone by the chancel wall with the words 'He stood between the Living and The Dead and the plague was stayed.'

> Visiting graveyards during daylight hours is quite different to visiting at night. People consider graveyards to be conducive to hypnotic

suggestion and fright, and 'the' most spooky places after dark, and after my night time visit to Eyam churchyard I am not going to argue! A night time visit is not for the squeamish.

We arrived at Eyam graveyard at 10 p.m. one November night and stood for a time at the front of the church by the side of the impressive tomb of Catherine Mompesson. Her ghost is said to wander between here and the church, and pause at the Celtic cross but I felt nothing. That may have been due to the three or four enormous spotlights that light the area. They are blinding and after looking in their direction, it causes blindness and a halo effect when viewing anything else. It was not until we walked round to the inky black graveyard at the back of the church that I started to experience the most bizarre and unaccountable sensations. I felt an increasing build up of pressure across my forehead and behind my ears as if I was wearing too tight a hat that was getting tighter and tighter by the second. I tried to be rational but my ears were drumming and my head was swimming. I knew that if I stayed there, I would pass out, but as soon as I decided to leave, the sensation vanished. Unknown to me, I was in the area where psychics have picked up strange vibrations and captured lots of orbs on camera. Orbs are light anomalies believed to be the first stage of ghost manifestation. I was not far from the place where people also regularly report seeing a little girl dancing round the gravestones.

Mechanics' Institute

Opposite the churchyard is the Mechanics Institute built in 1859, where many of the villagers learnt to read and write. It's now the village clubhouse with a concert room on the ground floor plus a bar and games room upstairs.

The Mechanics' Institute has a strange atmosphere

> I'd heard that the building had a strange atmosphere but when I spoke to the bar-tender who had worked there for nine years, I was told she'd never experienced anything. A few years ago when a cleaner was asked the same question she said she didn't believe in such things, yet the lady who had asked the question felt as if someone was behind her. Feeling rather uncomfortable, she mentioned this to the cleaner who laughed and said that her husband often said exactly the same. She then related a tale about when she was asked to work late. She was clearing up when she saw the curtains on the stage move as if children were playing about behind them, punching them. There was no draught and no-one else in the building, and this so freaked her that she never worked late again. Strange really, when she was adamant that she didn't believe in ghosts!

The Old Post Office

Almost all of the properties along this side of Church Street were rebuilt or refronted in the 18th and 19th century, and as we move along the street, the next property of interest is The Old Post Office.

During the plague, what is now the Old Post Office was the home of the Wragg family who were early victims of the plague. In more recent years it served as a post office but when it was being altered and sewerage excavations were being made in 1963, the gravestone of Alice Wragg was found under the floor. Although home internment was not unknown in the past, its more likely that for 300 years this stone served as a paving slab in the parlour.

Bagshawe House the home of the Siddall family

Next door is Bagshawe House, the home of the Siddall family during the plague. This true story from 1665 is the archetypal love story, a tale of doomed love with a final unexpected ghostly twist.

Emmot Siddall was a beautiful young woman who lived with her family in a thatched cottage in the heart of the village of Eyam. She was deeply in love with Rowland Torre the son of the flour-miller from the neighbouring village of Stoney Middleton, and like all young couples, they spent time together in simple pursuits just enjoying each other's company. But their brief spell of happiness was about to change for ever.

Directly opposite the Siddall's cottage, on September 7th 1665, George Vicars died an agonising death and as more deaths followed, the dreadful facts became clear; Eyam had been struck by the deadly plague.

The village chose to isolate itself to stop the plague spreading, and at a time when Rowland's reassuring presence would have helped ease the dire circumstances they were in, Emmot was detained in Eyam, forbidden to make any further contact with him for the foreseeable future.

The Siddall family was soon plunged into mourning when Emmot's sister Sarah was the fifth plague victim. A month later on October 11th Emmot's brother Richard was the thirteenth victim. On October 14th, her father died and the following day her sister Ellen was the seventeenth victim.

The Siddall's cottage opposite the churchyard

Week after week Rowland waited patiently on the Eyam boundary in the hope of seeing Emmot amongst the congregation at the open air church services held in The Delph. It was only through this kind of observation that he was able to gauge what was happening in the village, then as if luck was at last smiling upon them, she saw him standing there in the far distance and her heart leapt with joy.

Although they were banned from any form of contact, from then on they saw each other regularly on either side of Cutlet's Delph. It was compulsory to keep a vast void of land between them which made it impossible for them to say what was on their minds or whisper what was in their hearts, but as the weeks passed, Rowland was at least assured that Emmot was well.

On October 22nd another sister Elizabeth died followed by sister Alice two days later. Elizabeth Siddall had lost her

The lovers were forced to part

husband and five of her seven children in the first seven weeks of the plague, then for almost six months the Siddall household was free of the plague which must have been a tremendous relief for Elizabeth, Emmot and younger brother Joseph. During this time Emmot and Rowland 'met' regularly in the Delph and with renewed hopes, they made plans to marry during the following wakes week.

This might have been inspired by Emmot's mother Elizabeth marrying another Eyam resident, John Daniel on the 24th April 1666. It is also possible that a small wedding reception was held within the village and they unknowingly invited a plague victim who infected Emmot, because she died on April 30th, just five days after the wedding.

When Emmot failed to appear at the trysting place, Rowland began to fear the worst. He didn't want to believe when rumours of her death filtered through to him, but when the rumours were confirmed by her continual absence, Rowland was heart-broken. His worst fears had been confirmed.

This tragic love story of Emmot Siddall and Rowland Torre showing the young lovers meeting either side of a metaphorical stream is told in simple, graphic terms in the magnificent stained-glass Plague Window in Eyam Church. Yet that is not the end of the story?

> *A few years ago, during the open air church service in The Delph, a young girl in the congregation grew more and more agitated and kept pulling at her mother's sleeve.*
>
> *The mother mumbled a stern reprimand, determined not to be distracted, yet her daughter was very insistent.*
>
> *Eventually unable to bear it any longer, the girl hissed in her mother's ear. 'There's a woman in shapeless, old fashioned clothes watching us. She has long, black hair hanging loose round her shoulders and looks very sad. She's wandering around looking helplessly lost.'*
>
> *Thinking it was someone in costume, the mother was not unduly perturbed until she looked around and saw that everyone was muffled up against the cold and there was not a period costume in sight.*
>
> *'I think she's a ghost!' the girl whispered.*
>
> *So could this be Emmot Siddall returning to the Delph to try once more to make contact with Rowland her lost love.*

The Plague Cottages

Moving back across the road, next to the graveyard are the plague cottages.

Rose Cottage where nine members of the Thorpe family died, but do any come back in spirit as this photograph would indicate?

The end cottage on the plague row is the Hawksworth cottage. Peter Hawksworth was the third plague victim, buried on September 23rd. His wife Jane was three months pregnant and although she survived and later married William Ainsworth, another plague survivor, her fourteen month old son Humphrey died on October 17th — the 18th plague victim and her baby, born in March died after two days.

At the other end is Rose Cottage where nine members of the Thorpe family died between September 26th 1665 and May 2nd 1666.

In between these two cottages is Plague Cottage where it all began.

A former resident of Plague cottage, living there in retirement was a veteran soldier named Adam Holmes. While examining a defective flue in the kitchen one day, he found a pair of ancient leather stays concealed in a crevice in the chimney. His heart quailed as he gingerly withdrew the article of figure control from its place of hiding, and fearing that it might have been hidden there at the time of the plague he hastily buried the leather stays in the garden.

The front bedroom of Plague Cottage is said to be haunted by a pleasant faced lady in a blue smock. According to Wayne Anthony Bowlan, a former resident named Mrs Green told him about a haunting that happened to her late husband Bill in 1978. The cottage had two bedrooms and the Greens slept in the back bedroom. When their grandson stayed, they put him in the front bedroom, but he was not happy. He woke to find a lady standing by his bed watching him before simply fading away.

He woke to find a lady standing by his bed watching him before simply fading away

He refused to sleep there any more and insisted on moving into the back bedroom with his grandparents, but because it would have been too cramped for three, Bill moved into the front bedroom. A couple of nights later, he saw the apparition for the first time.

Bill was a down to earth, level headed man who was not prone to exaggeration or inventive story telling, so naturally he thought he'd been dreaming. The next time she appeared in the doorway of the room, and being wide awake, Bill got out of bed and went towards her at which point she simply vanished. Bill had seen her clearly enough to be able to describe her as being neatly dressed with a pleasant face. She wore her hair curled under with a fringe in a style he could only describe as old fashioned, a fact that was emphasised by the plain style of her navy blue dress. After seeing her for the fifth time and having had his sleep disturbed so often, he refused to sleep in the front bedroom ever again.

The Former Village Pond

After the plague cottages is a small green field that used to be the site of the village pond which was known as the Eaver. On the eastern churchside of the Eaver stood the village inn called The Shrewsbury Arms which in the mid 18th century was kept by William Wood's grandfather. It's no longer a pond and in the centre of this area is the roasting spit used at the village carnival time. The building behind the spit is a pigeon house in Eyam Hall gardens. This rare example dates from an age before refrigeration when fresh meat in winter was in very short supply. Fresh pigeon was a welcome addition to a diet of salted or dried meat.

The sheep roast used annually during Carnival Week at Eyam. This area was previously the village pond known as the Eaver

Eyam Hall

At the core of Eyam Hall is a Tudor Mansion that was originally the residence of the Brays of Eyam. It was purchased by Thomas Wright about the middle of the 17th century. A new front was erected and other alterations made around 1677 using materials from Bradshaw Hall. Some of the interior wainscoting has the initials F.B and J.B., with the date 1594 (or possibly 6) and an inverted stone on the outside with the initials M.B. This leaves us with the question, are these initials connected with the Bray or the Bradshaw families? There is a poem written on one of the panes of glass and on another someone has inscribed the crest and arms of the Wright family, an ownership that has stretched unbroken for over 300 years.

Eyam Hall

Eyam Hall opened its doors to the public in 1992, reflecting in its ambience the fact that this charming family owned manor house has been the much loved home of the Wright family for many years. It is one of the most welcoming houses in Derbyshire and a guided tour is highly recommended.

> What is also of great interest is the fact that Eyam Hall is haunted. At least three ghosts have been reported here. The late Granny Lowe recalled the ghost of an old man that was always seen sitting at a circular table in a top-storey room. The solution – to keep the door locked, a rather futile gesture, if it was supposed to keep a ghost inside.
>
> A young woman is reported to haunt a top floor bedroom. Dogs will not go into that room and often people in the street have seen her looking out of the third window from the left. Could this be the same ghostly lady who has been seen walking down the stairs?
>
> To celebrate hallowe'en, in 2008, the hall hosted a spooky 'Hallow Eyam' with creepy music, ghostly stories and eerie sound effects. According to Nichola Wright, most of the ghost stories are handed down over the years, but when asked if she believed in ghosts, she admitted – 'I'm not sure that I believe in ghosts but if there are any at Eyam Hall, they're happy ones as there is a lovely, friendly atmosphere here.'

> The courtyard of the hall houses a selection of craft shops and a tea room. It is closed by a solid gate but on one particular evening ghost walk as 17 people stood in the courtyard watching, the gate slowly closed, yet there was no wind and no one near.

The old laundry which is accessed through the courtyard is very spiritually active. It is actually built over a well which, disregarding the grid, is still open in the centre of the room. Apparently many years ago, when repairing the sides of the well, they discovered human bones and not knowing what to do with them, put them back. There is a story that a servant girl named Sarah Mills was drowned here in 1777 and ever since, this has caused strange sensations in the old laundry. It can be either very cold or very warm for no apparent reason, and people have felt like passing out.

The group that I visited with began commenting on the way their breath clouded, and to prove the point, people started huffing out balloons of cold breath. I didn't feel particularly cold, but the woman next to me started dithering and pacing round as if in major discomfort.

It was then that I started to feel a tightening in my chest and throat as if I was coming down with a cold. I had difficulty breathing due to a hot, damp atmosphere like you'd experience in a sauna, but this was cloggy and stale, the soiled, dusty smell of dirty, wet clothes, soapy washing water and clothes being boiled. Suddenly, I was transported back to my grand-mother's kitchen on wash-day. It wasn't just my imagination or the props like the boiler, dolly tub, rubbing board, poncher or pull up airer hanging from the high raftered ceiling.

I screwed up my nose in distaste and tried to cover my mouth but I had to get out of the place. The smell lingered with me until I moved outside into the fresh air. The obvious solution would be that earlier that day, some of the hall staff had put on a practical demonstration of how wash-days would have been conducted in Victorian times, yet I was assured that this laundry had never staged such demonstrations. I could therefore only conclude that somehow, like all other mysterious psychic phenomena, sprits are able to activate our sense of smell as a means of communicating with us.

In pre-mechanical days the horse was extremely valuable to its owner both as a form of transport and as a draught animal, so its not unusual to find many stories relating to the sound and sighting of spectral horses. Apparently a spectral white horse has been seen looking over the gate of Garden Croft near Eyam Hall. It's said that the horse is linked to the victim of an inheritance scandal, but why the horse should return in spirit is unclear.

The village green where you will find the stocks and the old market hall

The Village Green

Opposite the Hall is the village green on the edge of which stands a rather fine detached house, the only Georgian brick house in the village. It was used for a period as a hotel. A child was supposedly murdered there in the bedroom on the left of the building and his ghost is occasionally seen at the window.

On the opposite side of the green which was originally a cobbled area, is the original market hall, a small stone building where the farmers sold their produce.

> *This could also have been the site of a hostel for nursing the sick during the plague, as the clergymen advised that plague victims should be removed from their homes into huts or barracks built upon the common land.*

In the centre of the green are the village stocks restored in 1951 to mark the festival of Britain. Stocks were not introduced into English law until 1351 but by a statute of 1405, any village without a set of stocks could be downgraded to a hamlet. Not surprisingly few survive but this is a fine example. Those who refused to obey the law could be put in the stocks for all manner of petty crimes too numerous to mention, and in the 17th century, a further amendment was added to the already existing list of crimes punishable by a period in the stocks – 'Any person convicted of drunkenness should be fined 5s or spend six hours in the stocks'.

It obviously didn't cut out all crime because by 1808 crime had become such a problem that the Eyam and Stoney Middleton Society for the Prosecution of Felons was set up to keep law and order, a job which was handed over to the modern police force in 1857.

Look through the railings behind the stocks into the Delph or Delf. *This natural hollow was both an open–air church and the setting for one of our most poignant love stories associated with the plague – the story of Emmot and Rowland. William Wood also referred to two or three head-stones that once existed in the Delph, to the memory of the Wraggs, but they are now lost without trace.*

Also of interest is a strip of land in the Delph known as the Toothill. This is claimed to be the site of an ancient Celtic altar or shrine consecrated by the Druids to the worship of Teutates, or Tuisti, the Celtic god of war whose name survives in our Tuesday.

Continue along the main road, passing the current post office on your right then Laburnum Cottage, reputedly one of the oldest buildings in Eyam

Next is the cottage where Margaret Blackwell had a miraculous recovery from the plague.

> *Anthony Blackwell the Eyam stonemason and his wife Margaret died just before Christmas 1665, leaving their two children Francis and Margaret. It wasn't long before fourteen year old Margaret started feeling ill and stayed in bed while Francis prepared his breakfast bacon. When he had finished, he poured the fat into a wooden piggin (jug). This would later be used in cooking or making rush lights for illumination. Francis left the house and while away, Margaret alone and in much pain, went in search of something to ease her unquenchable thirst. She picked up the jug and began to drink the warm fat which must have made her very sick, but on his return, Francis found her much better and stronger. Margaret eventually recovered fully and lived to a ripe old age.*

Richard Furness, a neighbour and renowned in Eyam as a poet, wrote about the episode -

> *But nature rallied, and her flame still burn'd –*
> *Sunk in the socket, glimmer'd and returned;*
> *The golden bowl and silver cord were sound;*
> *The cistern's wheel revolved its steady round;*
> *Fire- vital fire – evolved the living stream,*
> *And life's fine engine pump'd the purple stream.*

The cottage to the left of Pursgloves Butchers shop is said to be haunted. Former residents used to hear footsteps approaching and the door would unlatch and swing open, but the footsteps never crossed the threshold. It happened so often that the ghost was a nuisance. When the cottage was extended, that doorway was sealed and a new entrance made, but the ghost continued to walk down the garden path and past the house.

Hall Hill troughs established in 1558

Hawkhill – named after the sport of falconry enjoyed here by the Staffords and Bradshaws

When reaching Hawkhill Road, turn right and go up Hawkhill Road. Hawkhill takes its name from the Bradshaw's indulgence in the popular sport of falconry carried out in this area.

On your left are Hall Hill Troughs so called because of the nearby Bradshaw Hall. They formed part of a series of troughs established in 1558, many of which still remain.

Next to the troughs is the Methodist Chapel and

The Museum with the ruins of Bradshaw Hall behind

the Eyam Museum. Note the weather vane on the roof with the black rat, the cause of that dreadful plague. A visit to Eyam Museum is highly recommended. It tells the moving story of the plague and the tragic tales of real people who sacrificed their lives to protect their neighbours. Opening hours are late March to early November, Tuesday to Sunday. 01433 631371

Behind the Museum standing on rising ground at the north-west of the village is the ruined Bradshaw Hall. It stands on the same site and incorporates part of the earlier Stafford Hall.

The Staffords and their strange tenure

LEFT: *Bradshaw Hall incorporates part of the earlier Stafford Hall*
CENTRE: *A stained glass window depicting St Helen*
RIGHT: *St Helen's lamp*

Although some historian now believe that the Staffords acquired their land through marriage with the Furnivals, for many generations, the Staffords of Stafford Hall were a very wealthy family who owned much land and property around Eyam. According to old deeds, this was granted to the first of the Staffords by King John, but on certain specified conditions; they must keep a lamp permanently burning on the altar of St Helen's Church, Eyam. (This was later incorporated into the present church dedicated to Saint Lawrence.) St Helen was born around 270AD and was the mother of Constantine who later became the first Christian Emperor.

This would seems no big deal for a wealthy family with many servants to do such a task, but this peculiar tenure stated that the procedure should be supervised by the actual male possessor or his heir. In default of male issue, an heiress could perform the task provided that she was unmarried, because on her death or marriage, all the land would pass from the family back to the crown.

Stafford Hall is said to have been built during the reign of Henry V1 (1422-1461), and has been described as a spacious and massive building, the greatest proportions being in length. In the interior the rooms were all floored with black oak, which although of a mirror like brightness, contributed to the sombre, gloomy appearance which was principally caused by the narrow windows. From the middle of the principal or southern front of the exterior of the mansion projected a large circular stone on which was carved the Staffords family arms – a chevron between three martlets

Around the middle of the 16th century, it was the home of Humphrey Stafford. He had five daughters Margaret, Alice, Gertrude, Ann and Katherine, but his two sons Humphrey and Roland had died in their youth. His wife had also died and despite the fact that Humphrey Stafford needed a legitimate male heir to inherit his vast estates, he had no wish to remarry. Katherine had married Rowland Morewood of Bradford, Yorkshire; Gertrude had married a lineal ancestor of the Earl of Newburgh, Hassop; Alice married John Savage of Castleton, Ann married Francis Bradshaw, but Margaret refused all suitors and remained at Stafford Hall with her father. Between them they tended the lamp on the altar of St Helen's Church.

It was March 1565 when they received news that the unfortunate Mary, Queen of Scots (1542-87) had just arrived under house arrest at Chatsworth House, and they made plans to visit Chatsworth to show their respect. They were able to see the royal visitor, and their loyalty and admiration for the captive queen left a deep impression. As the Earl of Shrewsbury and his wife Bess of Hardwick remained her captor until 1584, the Stafford probably saw the captive Queen on various occasions, and in an age when people communicated regularly through letters, it was understandable that Margaret should write about her concern for the plight of the

Mary Queen of Scots who impressed Margaret Stafford enough to write to Anthony Babington expressing her loyalty and admiration for the lady

unfortunate queen. One such letter was sent to her friend Anthony Babington.

The years passed, and as Humphrey Stafford advanced in years Margaret undertook the daily task of attending to the lamp that burnt day and night on the altar of St Helen Church, then one evening just before dusk, Margaret took a stroll along the secluded dell known as The Delph, just below Stafford Hall. For some time she sat in deep contemplation, her head bowed, but when she raised her head a figure dressed in white was gliding silently towards her and in each hand she held a burning lamp. As they faced each other, the woman lifted the lights and Margaret saw with indescribable horror that she was not of this world –

Margaret saw with indescribable horror that she was not of this world

> *Her motionless lips were still as death,*
> *her words came forth without her breath.*
> *There rose not a heave from her bosom's swell*
> *and there seemed not a pulse in her veins to dwell.*
> *Though her eyes shone out, yet the lids were fixed,*
> *and the glance that it gave was wild and unmix'd*
> *with ought of change, as the eyes may seem,*
> *of the restless who walk in a troubled dream.*
>   SIEGE OR CORINTH

Margaret Stafford heard the unearthly voice which seemed to her like the voice of her own soul speaking in the calm of thought –

> *Tonight fair lady I come unto thee,*
> *with tidings most sad – fate's changeless decree.*
> *Dark troubles await thee lady alas,*
> *I see them in future coming to pass.*
> *Of an ancient race – the last of the name,*
> *Oh! Lady of sorrow I was the same*
> *And many the perils I travelled through,*
> *Oh daughter of Stafford, e'en so must you*

Of dangers here long, ah thou must beware.
No sire wilt thou have, they sufferings to share
Nay! Round him again, no more shalt though cling;
his spirit e'en now is fast on the wing.

Having imparted her message, the spectre slowly vanished, and Margaret hurried back to the hall to be greeted with the news that her father had just died. A cloud of deep despondence overshadowed the village and in a large tapestried room at Stafford Hall, the last of that name was laid in his coffin of black oak before being carried to the village church. There, the coffin was carried once round the cross in the belief that this would procure a more speedy release of the soul from purgatory – a Popish custom which was practiced long after the Reformation, even by Protestants. Finally Humphrey Stafford was laid beneath the northern aisle of the little church.

After the funeral, many of the villagers went to the Shrewsbury Arms which stood at the east end of the Eaver – the pond at the centre of the village, now the site of the annual sheep roast. It was kept at this time by Lawrence Decket, a blacksmith and the sign board on each side bore a rudely painted, large Talbot dog.

It was here about two years later, in 1585 that a messenger arrived in some haste. After talking to Decket, they both hurried up to Stafford Hall where the messenger handed Margaret Stafford a letter from Anthony Babington. Prior to his arrest and subsequent torture and death, Anthony Babington with a purse of gold had induced a friend to warn Margaret Stafford that the letter which she had written to him expressing her deep sympathy for Mary Queen of Scots after seeing her at Chatsworth, had been found amongst the Queen's papers at Chertsey. Her enemies had decided that the Staffords were involved in the conspiracy to free her and there was a warrant out for their arrest.

The faithful Decket helped conceal Margaret Stafford in the Salt Pan, a very secluded, long, deep chasm in the Delph where it would be impossible for anyone not acquainted with the labyrinth to find her. Hardly an hour had passed before four armed men arrived in Eyam and dismounted at Stafford Hall with a warrant for the arrest of both Humphrey and Margaret Stafford. They were informed of the death of the master but that made them even more determined to find the mistress of the house. They ransacked the hall, searched every property in the village and threatened the people with instant death if they did not disclose the whereabouts of Miss Stafford. No one but Decket knew where she was, and true to his word, at the first opportunity he conveyed her away to an isolated cottage at Gother Edge (now Gotherage) on the edge of Eyam Moor. The word gother is Celtic and means red or red edge – quite descriptive of this place. For eighteen years this poor, unhappy woman lived in hiding, but at dead of night, when she had ascertained that her pursuers were absent from the place, she ventured back into the village where she would visit the church to tend the lamp of St Helen.

It was not until the death of Queen Elizabeth in 1603 that it was safe for Margaret Stafford to return to Stafford Hall, by which time she was a shadow of her former self. Her plight was related to the king who asked how she could be recompensed for her years of depravation, and she humbly requested the annulment of the tenure by which her forefathers had held their land at Eyam, the tending of the lamp of St Helen. The monarch ordered that to be done immediately and the lands of the Staffords were to be inherited in fee simple, by the co-heiresses of Humphrey Stafford and their heirs for ever.

Margaret Stafford became a much loved village benefactor and amongst her other works of charity, she erected the church's new tower and four bells. A bell dating from 1628 is still one of the six bells. Margaret Stafford was interred beside her father near the northern aisle of the church, and thanks to her, Stafford Hall passed to her sister Anne, daughter and co-heriess of Humphrey Stafford who in 1565 had married Francis Bradshaw, family of the notorious Judge John Bradshaw who sentenced Charles I to death.

It was their great grandson, also named Francis who around 1611 built a three storey extension on the east side of Stafford Hall and changed the name to Bradshaw Hall.

There is every possibility that it was partially destroyed during the Civil War because sadly it never appeared to be the Bradshaw's family home after that. When plague broke out in 1665 the widow and daughter of Squire George Bradshaw left Eyam permanently for Brampton in Yorkshire.

According to some reports, the fabric of the building was used by Thomas Wright to build Eyam Hall around 1677. Some of the interior wainscoting at Eyam Hall has the initials F.B and J.B., with the date 1594 (or possible 6) and an inverted stone on the outside with the initials M.B. Could this FB be Francis Bradshaw

For a period of time, the reduced Bradshaw Hall was occupied by other

The ruins of Bradshaw Hall

families then converted into a cotton mill, when it was seriously damaged by fire. According to *The History and Antiquities of Eyam,* by the early 19th century it was greatly dilapidated and used as a barn. In 1961 there was subsidence of the south-west corner of the building and in 1962, the corner fell away. It was necessary to demolish all the unsafe stonework leaving only the northern corner, the façade that faces the museum today. In 2006 an excavation confirmed this and revealed fragments of 17th and 18th century pottery, bone and glass that are now on display in the museum. The lamp of St Helen still hangs in the vestry, and some years ago, the Staffords pew was made into the screen which now encloses the belfry.

It's now almost impossible to visualise how impressive this building must once have been when all we have left is a crumbling ruin and a handful of ghosts.

Opposite is the main village car park, which is the end of this walk.

2: Mompesson's Well

1½ miles (2·45km)

This walk is ideal to combine with *Walk 1*, but it's outlined separately because it's outside the village and has steep climbs. It is however suitable for wheelchair/buggy users and helpers with stamina. Information from the plague are in italics, ghost stories are in boxes.

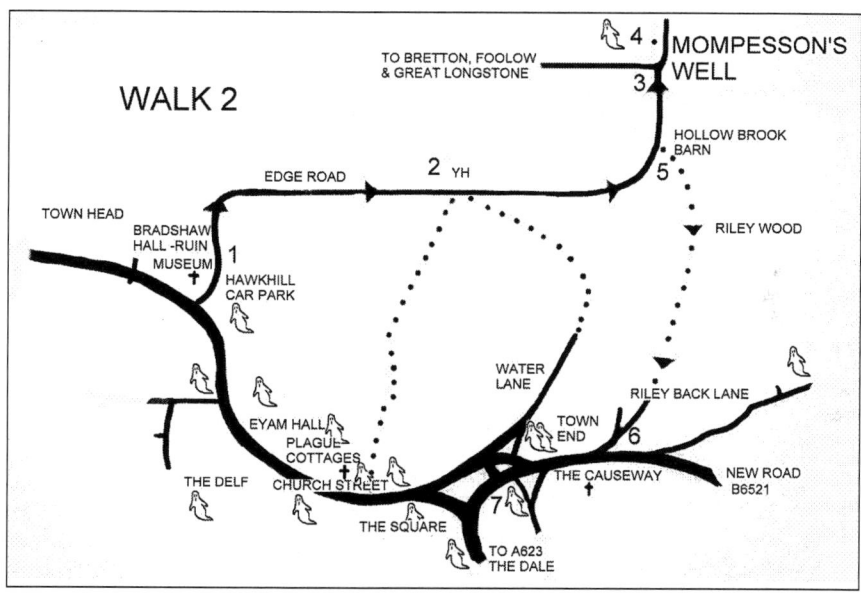

The Walk
Leave the Hawkhill car park by the entrance – 1. Directly opposite is the museum behind which is the ruined Bradshaw Hall (see *Walk 1* for details).

Turn right and walk up Hawkhill Road. Continue up the hill heading north ignoring the lane going off to the left. Continue up the road which changes from Hawkhill Road to Edge Road. This might seem like a gradual climb along a quiet country road but with no pavements, take care. After a short distance, you will pass a house on your left set back from the road – 2. This was the former village poor-house where the paupers of the parish suffered pain, misery and humiliation in their declining years.

The ruins of Bradshaw Hall

William Wood the Eyam chronicler referred to several plague memorial stones recording the deaths of people named Whiteley, behind and to the west end of these buildings, but they are no longer there.

It was written that after the plague, William Mompesson personally supervised the destruction of all materials calculated to conceal germs. Furniture, clothing and bedding were burnt on huge bonfires, but 100 years later, Anna Seward suggested that the word could have been 'buried' rather than 'burned'. She came to this assumption when in 1757, five cottagers were digging in the heathy moorland above Eyam which was used as a graveyard during the plague.

According to Miss Seward, they came across something which had the appearance of having once been 'linen' and conscious of their situation, hastily buried it again. Within a few days all five cottagers sickened and three died. As more people died, the people of Eyam were terrified that a new epidemic of the deadly plague had been awakened from the dust in which it had slumbered for ninety one years.

Miss Seward's information was obtained from a Dr Holland who put the number of dead at seventy, but according to William Wood, Miss Seward was misinformed. There was no corroborative evidence to support this claim and the mortality rate of that year was normal.

Subsequent writers have again questioned the handwriting. Could the word 'burned' have been 'buried', and just to confuse the issue further, could the word 'linen' have been 'lime'? Lime was used in the interment of un-coffined corpses.

Mompesson's Well

A little further along is Beech House, a large substantial house which is now a youth hostel opposite which are two footpaths leading back to Eyam – one via Water Lane, the other through St Lawrence's churchyard. To continue our walk, remain on the main road and after about ½ mile, ignore the road to your left sign posted to Bretton, Gt Hucklow, Foolow – 3, then after approximately 150 metres, on the left and just off the road is Mompesson's Well – 4.

The ghost of a young boy is said to haunt Mompesson's Well

> Mompesson's well was one of the boundary stones used like a market stone during the plague. It consists of a trough hewn out of stone which has been designed with the addition of a canopy of stone.
>
> The buyers were not able to touch any of the articles before purchase, but when the agreement was finalised, they would take the goods and deposit the money in the shallow waters of the trough. The ghost of a bewildered small boy is said to linger around here. Could he be from the plague era sent to collect some necessary supplies?

This area is known as Eyam Edge, which forms part of a chain of gritstone cliffs to the east of the River Derwent. Eyam has been described as geologically eccentric, and partial to variety, spreading itself over several different strata – limestone, shale and sandstone, capped with millstone grit. This area along Eyam Edge bears the scars of lead mining following the discovery in 1717 of the rich lead bearing vein, but the area was not new to lead mining. The first colonists to settle in the area were undoubtedly attracted by the lead. The Romans exploited this and sent huge consignments back to Rome. As well as extending natural caverns, the early lead miners worked the 'rakes' or surface veins, and coins and fragments of coarse pottery have been found on their spoil heaps.

Late 19th century lead miners

If you look W. NW you will see the chimneys of Ladywash Mine that relate to a story told by the late Clarence Daniel. A bath full of clay from Ladywash Mine was being soaked in preparation for making the annual Eyam well-dressings, and quite by chance he picked up a knob of the clay to discover that embedded in it was a small wooden pipe known as an acorn pipe because that is what the bowl resembles.

Such pipes were common a century or two ago, and superstitious miners often left votive offerings like this pipe in the underground workings of the mine for the T'Owd man, a strange figment of Peak

District lead mining lore. Lead miners looked on T'Owd Man as the collective spirit of the mine and their own predecessors, and he was offered great respect. T'Owd man's domain was the dark and dangerous subterranean world of the miners, and abandoned workings in particular.

The acorn pipe is now on display at the Eyam museum.

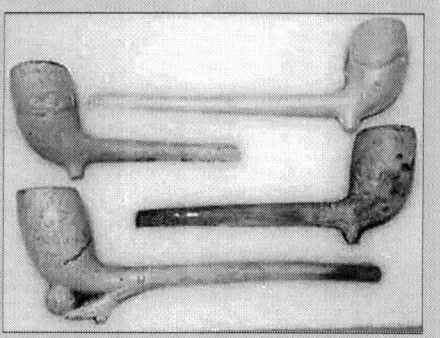

Pipes like these in Eyam Museum were left in the lead mines to placate T'Owd man

Leave Mompesson's Well and return to Edge Road. Turn right (south) along Edge Road, passing the Bretton junction on your right – 3 and a few metres further on your left just past Hollow Brook Barn, go through a squeeze stile onto a footpath with a sign into Riley Wood – 5. Wheelchair/buggy users must remain on the road to return to the village as this path is unsuitable.

Where the path divides, take the right hand path going down. This pleasant woodland path meanders down for ½ mile, eventually reaching a lane which bears round to the right into Riley Back Lane to arrive at The Causeway, part of the B6521-6. On your right and set back slightly from the road is Burch Row; on your left is Burch Place built around 1860. These cottages were the homes and workplaces of the villagers employed in silk weaving and cotton spinning. The clack and clatter of looms gave a measure of modest prosperity to the villagers working in their own homes in these cottage industries, but by the end of the 18th century, unable to cope with the mechanical processes and water power supplied by the rivers, these industries had declined.

On the opposite side of the road is the Wesleyan Chapel built in 1787. Turn right and on reaching The Square – 7, join Walk One through the village and back to the car park on Hawkhill Road which is the start/end of this walk.

3: Eyam to Foolow

A RESIDENT GHOST – SUPERSTITIOUS MINERS & SMOKING SPIRIT

3½ miles (5·65k)

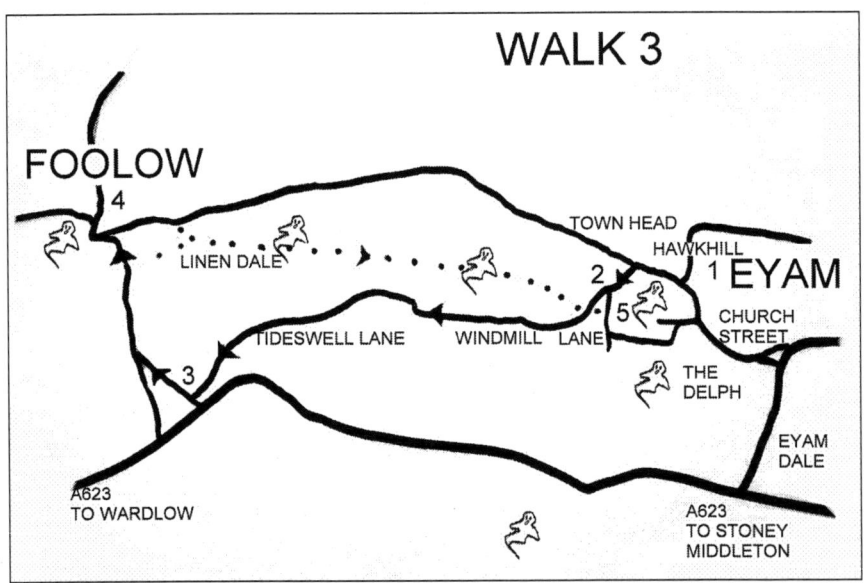

The Walk

Leave the Hawkhill car park by the entrance – 1. Directly opposite is the museum behind which is the ruined Bradshaw Hall (see *Walk 1* for details). Turn left and walk down to the main road. At the junction, turn right going up the slight slope towards Townhead. This area is known as Orchard Bank

During the plague, a woman living in the area of Orchard Bank, decided to go to Tideswell, one of the principle market towns of the Peak, frequented on market days by great numbers of people from the neighbouring villagers. Although the people of Eyam were expected to stay within the boundaries of the village, she had every confidence that she could mingle with the crowds unrecognised, and having walked the five miles, the first obstacle was getting past the watch set up on the eastern entrance of Tideswell. It was their job to stop and question all who passed that way, and to prevent anyone from Eyam entering the place on any business whatsoever.

'The Plague! The Plague! A woman from Eyam!' they all shouted

'Whence comest though?' asked the watch authoritively.

'From Orchard Bank,' she replied.

'And where be that?' the watch asked.

'Why verily,' said the woman, ''tis in the land of the living.'

The watch, not being familiar with the area allowed her to pass, but she had scarcely reached the market when she was recognised.

'A woman from Eyam,' someone cried and the call resounded from all sides.

'The plague! The plague! A woman from Eyam.'

People started pelting her with stones, mud, sods and other missiles, forcing the poor woman to turn and run. The mob followed her until she was miles out Tideswell and she returned to Eyam, bruised and battered from her ordeal.

Continue up the road to the junction of Little Edge where Fiddlers Bridge lies beneath the road. Turn to your right just before the Royal Oak Inn, now a private house. The building has had extensive alterations over the years but the original inn was built in 1587 and called The Heart of Oak. It was rebuilt in 1660 and renamed the Royal Oak as a mark of

The dressed well at Townhead and a detailed section, depicting part of the plague story

respect to the restoration of the monarchy.

Turn left just before the Royal Oak Inn. The Y junction ahead is the site of the Town Head Well dressing.

Little Edge is the right branch which leads round to Audrey Cottages, a long row of cottages that in 1808 may have been a cotton spinning mill housing 100 workers. In 1857 this was Froggatt's silk weaving establishment, later to be a boot and shoe factory, but is now dwelling houses.

Go back to the main road, and walk along the front of the cottages adjoining the Royal Oak.

At the end, protruding into the road is Merrill House, the 17th century home of Humphrey and Anne Merrill. Humphrey was the village herbalist at the time of the plague who would rely upon a storehouse of natural products and recipes passed down through the generations. The inventiveness of the village herbalist was astonishing yet many of the recipe left more than a little to chance.

Humphrey Merrill would have relied heavily upon advise given by The Plague Approved Physician that stated that to stay healthy – 'all should studiously avoid dancing, running,

Merrill House, home of the village herbalist during the plague

leaping about, lechery and baths'. Another profound piece of information stated that the plague 'never attempted the premises of tobacconists, tanners or shoemakers'.

The following are the kind of things Humphrey Merrill would have prescribed.

Cures for the plague sickness

Take barberries when they are ripe, steep them in warm water that the husks or outward skin may come off, then dry them that they may be beaten to a powder with a little salt, and when you find yourself somewhat discomposed, mix this powder with strong vinegar, about two drams in half a quarter of a pint and drink it up warm, and keep yourself warm also, that you may sweat upon it, but if you find yourself shivering with cold, you must take the powder in strong wine.

* * *

Take a great onion, hollow it, put in a fig, rue cut small and a dram of Venice treacle; put it close stuffed in wet paper, and roast it in the embers; apply it hot under the tumour.

* * *

A Most Excellent Drink Against The Plague

Take three gills of the best Malmsey; boil it till one pint be boiled away; put thereto long pepper, ginger and nutmeg beaten....let all these boil together. Put in one ounce of Mithridatum and two ounces of Venice Treacle and a quarter pint of aqua vitae. Take morning and evening one spoonful. There never was man, woman or child that this drink deceived.

* * *

The Best Pill Generally Under Heaven

Take the best yellow aloes, two ounces myrrh and saffron, of each one ounce; beat them together in a mortar a good while.
Put in a little sweet wine then roll it up and of this make five pills. Take on a day next your heart, a scruple more and it will expulse the pestilence that day.

* * *

Plague Sickness

Take water of scabious, endive, rue and red roses, of each four ounces; white *dittany, tormentile, white coral, gentian, and bole armoniack, with terra figillita; reduce those that are to be powdered separately. Infuse them in the water in a glass vessel and drink about an ounce at a time, pretty warm. Keep the body warm after it.*

* * *

Plague Sickness
Take a viol or some other glass and fill it to the third part with Venice Treacle, the other third part with brandy or spirit of wine; mix these well together by shaking, and take morning and evening half an ounce in two ounces of mint, rue or balm water.

* * *

Contagious Distemper
This occurs as a very much approved remedy.
Take walnuts when the green husk is on them, and before the shell is hardened underneath; put them when bruised into white wine eight days; then with some balm, rue and tops of feverfew, and wormwood a little bruised, put them into an alembick, and distil them; then when you drink and ounce and a half of the water, which you may do morning, noon and night, put in some perfumed confits, and stir them well about until they are dissolved.

* * *

If there be a blotch appear, take a pigeon and pluck the feathers off her tail very bare, and set her tail to the sore, and she will draw out the venom till she die. Apparently if no pigeon was at hand, a chicken, frog or toad would do the same service of drawing out the 'venom'.

Anne Merrill survived the plague but sadly Humphrey's remedies didn't prevent him dying from the plague in September 1666.

Next to Merrill House is Furness House which had previously been known as Olde House. It dates from 1615 and the change of name was because it was the birthplace on August 2nd 1791 of Richard Furness. He was renowned in Eyam as a poet who wrote 30 carols and was called the Poet Laureate of the Peak. The house is still in family hands.

If you walk past Furness House, you'll find an unsigned public footpath.

This leads through the farmyard of Hollins Farm to the field where Humphrey Merrill, the herbalist is buried. The spot is marked by a table tomb.

Another member of the Merrill family named Andrew lived at Hollins House, and survived the plague by going to the edge of Eyam Moor and building a crude hut in which he lived with his pet cockerel until the plague was over

Furness House

Continue a little further until reaching Townhead where the road branches. On your right is the last house in the village now known as Townhead House, but formerly the Townhead Inn.

Ahead of you is the 1733 building, established as a factory for silk weaving, a process that had originated from Macclesfield through a Tideswell agency. Eyam appealed to the silk manufacturers as a location because of lower wages compared to Macclesfield. Initially the Eyam weavers collected their raw materials and returned the finished goods to Tideswell, but later materials came direct from Macclesfield and the carters stayed overnight at the Townhead Inn. If you look up at the building you'll see a dovecot on the end wall. It is said that this was used to house carrier pigeons which took messages direct between Eyam and Macclesfield.

This industry may have made a gradual decline if it hadn't been for an Eyam weaver named Ralph Wain. He could neither read nor write, yet he devoted all his leisure

The former Townhead Inn, the last house in the village

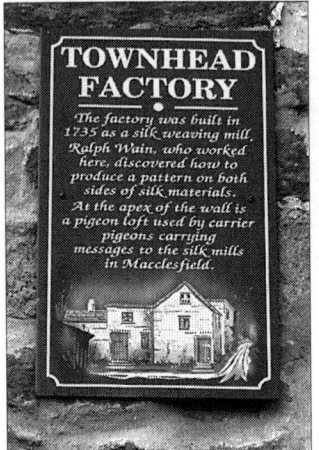 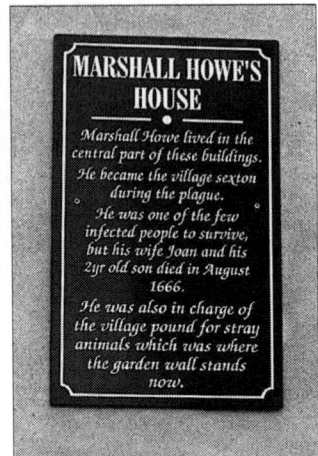

Information plaques like these are displayed all around the village

time to experimenting with various weaving principles until after many disappointments, in 1785 he discovered a revolutionary process whereby the designs and motifs could be reproduced on both sides of the material.

His employers must have been absolutely delighted and in order to capitalise on the discovery, offered Ralph Wain an executive post with the firm. A man of shy and retiring disposition, he refused. He had achieved what he set out to do and renounced any honours attached to the invention when the Macclesfield company patented the idea.

Specimens of Eyam silk are still treasured possessions in the village. Some are displayed in the museum together with tools and shuttles used in their manufacture.

Turn the corner into Tideswell Lane and immediately on your left is a completely transformed cottage that during the plague belonged to Marshall Howe.

> *Marshall Howe was a sturdy lead miner who claimed exemption from the plague because he had recovered from a slight infection – the principle on which vaccination is based. He then turned his survival to good use by appointing himself the villager sexton and gravedigger. Historical press has not been kind to Howe, accusing him of being greedy and grasping while profiting from the distress of others. He displayed a morbid audacity and impudence in relieving plague victims of their possession in*

payment for his services, compensating himself for his ghoulish work by rifling the homes of those he had buried. The way he made claim to their goods and chattels with such temerity created a sense of awe and astonishment amongst the people. In the village ale house in post-plague days he would entertain the company by boasting about his illicit plunder adding that he had – 'pinners and napkins enough to kindle his pipe while he lived'.

He was however cheated of the spoils when he was informed that a man called Unwin had just died. Howe hurriedly dug a shallow grave then ascended the stairs to the chamber where Unwin lay. He soon had the corpse on his back and was just descending the stairs when the supposedly dead man, in a kind of half-smothered rattle in his throat said – 'I want a posset!'

Howe dropped the man and ran, Unwin got his posset and made a full recovery.

Posset is a mulled ale and was a favourite Derbyshire drink consumed on Christmas eve or given as an aphrodisiac to newly weds on their wedding night. It was also drunk during the Eyam plague as the medicinal properties of posset were well documented at that time. Into the warm ale is added spices like ginger and nutmeg, a sweetener like syrup or honey, an egg and cream. Some people added a dash of rum or other spirit, plus a slice of bread, toasted until it

The posset cup in Eyam Museum

Will this man soon be requiring the services of Marshall Howe? No it's all part of the 2009 Eyam Carnival parade

was a uniform straw colour, then broken into the posset jug and soaked with the liquid.

Leave Eyam – 2 – and continue up Tideswell Lane which after the last bungalow becomes more like a winding track.

This would have been the route taken by the woman from Eyam when she decided to go to Tideswell during the plague.

The village of Foolow where stone cottages cluster round the village green and the duck pond, complete with ducks

Follow this undulating, walled track for about 1¼ mile until reaching the road junction – 3. To your left is the A623, but turn right and follow the road for approximately half a mile to reach Foolow – 4.

Foolow is another name like Highlow where the 'low' is actually from 'hlaw' meaning a hill. Foo could be the name of a Saxon farmer, or some sources say Foolow means multi-coloured hill. It appears to have no connection with the local village idiot although over to the west is a dry limestone valley called Silly Dale.

This is an area divided by dry stone walls which vary in composition throughout the Peak District. Here, the white and grey limestone walls that divide up the patchwork of fields glow white in the sunlight, in comparison to the darker, flatter rocks in the gritstone areas.

Foolow is the quintessential Peak Land village with stone cottages that cluster around a village green and duck pond complete with ducks.

Some say it's not a duck pond, but a ducking pond where scolds and witches were ducked as a form of punishment. The accused was strapped to a chair on the end of a plank and lowered into the pond. The amount of dips and the extent of time in the water depended upon the severity of the crime.

Another reminder of our barbarous past is the bull ring, also positioned on the village green at the foot of a 14th century stepped cross.

Like the one in the square in Eyam these bull-rings are now rare examples from a time when bulls were tethered to be baited and attacked by dogs namely the bull-dogs and bull-terriers.

The village cross, although not old in comparison to the 8th century

Saxon cross in Eyam churchyard was erected in its present position in 1868 after removal from the locality of the Wesleyan Reform Chapel. The cross was employed in every sacred ritual, designed to excite sentiments of piety or compassion and reverence. Originally placed by the wayside, these crosses served as boundary markers and were used by itinerate priests and monks to preach from. The cross was frequently placed on the highway to deter highwaymen and restrain other predators in the same way that in the market place, the market cross was a signal for upright intentions and fair dealings.

At the heart of Foolow is the 14th century cross and bull ring

Many of these crosses in public places were removed and destroyed by an Act of Parliament in 1643, but local citizens circumvented the wishes of parliament by concealing these crosses with the intention of re-erecting them when the government policy changed, which it was likely to do at short notice during the Civil War.

Foolow is only two miles west of Eyam, but Mary Buxton who died in March 1666 appears to have been the only plague death here.

Jenny was a young, single mother when she bought a cottage in Foolow, but didn't realise that it came complete with ghost. At least, she assumed it was a ghost after she had eliminated all other possible explanations. When she had female friends staying all was well, nothing unusual happened but when male friends stayed, they found great difficulty sleeping and even had their bed-clothes torn off by an unseen presence. It was when she was researching the history of the cottage that Jenny made a rather surprising discovery. According to the deeds, in the 19th century a single lady had owned the cottage, something that was quite unusual in those days. Was it this lady who was keeping a motherly eye on Carol and acting as an unseen chaperone?

Leave the village green and walk down towards the Bull's Head Inn which you pass on your left as you head out of the village. After about 200 yards down the Eyam Road, immediately after the Foolow village sign, you'll find a wall stile on your right. Follow the footpath through the field bearing very slightly left towards a ruined barn. Continue alongside the wall on your right, over stiles and down into the valley of Linen Dale where you'll find a sign post to Eyam beside a squeeze stile. Evidence of pre-historic and Roman occupation has been found in Linen Dale; fragments of Derbyshire ware, a lead spindle whorl, weapons of chipped flint, local chert and polished stones.

The road down past the Bull's Head on your left

Bear slightly left up the grassy bank, over a wall and across the next field to a wall gate. Go through the gate then head across the next field and through another wall gate. Keep walking straight on in an easterly direction to cross an overall total of nineteen small fields separated by stiles, broken and gated walls.

This area is dotted with old lead mines. Lead miners were great believers in the importance of dreams that could foretell the whereabouts of rich veins, and at a mine just west of Eyam, a miner decided to sell his mine despite a voice in his head that encouraged him to persevere in his quest for lead.

'Go on there's ore,' persisted the voice but eventually the miner's patience gave up and he sold his title to another miner who almost immediately made a rich strike of ore. Dreams could also forecast danger. A mine owner once ordered all his men out of the workings following a vivid dream of disaster. Later that day, the mine shaft collapsed.

Old lead miners were a very superstitious lot

> Nellie Kirkham, an authority on Derbyshire lead mines tells of a ghost that haunts Hanging Flatt Mine near Eyam. He has been seen underground and on the surface carrying a spade over his shoulder. He wanders along the old workings muttering to himself and oblivious to onlookers. Mrs E. Haythornewaite who owned the derelict Needham Farm above the mine, claimed that she had often heard the strokes of a pick within the closed mine. Miners believe that these sounds and every other thing that happens in the mines are caused by the Knockers or little people who inhabit the subterranean depths.

After the last stile, walk along a narrow hedged and walled path between houses to go down steps into Tideswell Lane. Cross the lane diagonally left to go through a wall gap, then walk across the field corner to go through another wall gap bringing you out on Windmill Lane – 5. Turn right and a few hundred yards along here was the site of the village windmill which ground the local grain. There was an old tradition amongst miller called 'blooding the mill'. At midnight on St Martin's Eve (November 10th) the miller would kill a cock and sprinkle its blood over the machinery in the belief that he would then be protected from accidents in the coming year.

The windmill was pulled down in 1875 and the stone was used to build the village school. The only evidence of its existence, apart from the name of this lane, is a 15" x10" painting by John Plant made in September 1874 which now hangs in Eyam museum. Almost one hundred years later, John Plant's painting was converted into the 1961 village well dressing.

The village windmill by John Plant

The painting clearly shows the windmill with an adjacent barn and cottage, and when the adjoining barn was converted into a house, the owner commenting that 'all the cracks and crannies were full of grain'. There's now an abandoned grinding stone on the site and if you look closely, you

The 1981 well dressing of the windmill

might just detect a circular patch that identifies where the windmill stood.

Continue down Windmill Lane then turn left to go down Dunlow Lane until reaching the junction with Cussy Lane. Turn left. At this point it is possible to see over a low stone wall into the Delph which also used to be called Cussy Delph.

This natural hollow was the open–air church where services were held during the time of the plague.

On the last Sunday in August 1765, to mark the centenary of the outbreak of the plague, Rev. Thomas Seward stood where Mompesson had stood in The Delph and preached a sermon as he had done. There was also a service to mark the bicentenary, and since 1910, the service in its present form has been conducted every year. The day has become known as Plague Sunday. This is also the setting for one of our most poignant love stories associated with the plague – the story of Emmot and Rowland, and William Wood also referred to two or three head-stones to the memory of the Wraggs that once existed here, but are now lost without trace.

There is also a strip of land in the Delph known as the Toothill which is claimed to be the site of an ancient Celtic altar or shrine consecrated by the Druids to the worship of Teutates, or Tuisti, the Celtic god of war whose name survives in our Tuesday.

Cross the road which has been skirting a small housing development called New Close. While serving as a war-time allotment a number of ancient artefacts were found. When foundations were being prepared for the first houses on this estate about fifty years ago, a Roman coin and fragments of coarse grey earthenware were dug up and residents have uncovered more finds since. One guy unearthed a lead spindle whorl and a perforated stone adze, but could this area hold other secrets? According to a recent newspaper report, there is also a ghostly presence.

> Apparently Hannah and Gordon Robinson are fuming at the antics of a pipe smoking ghost who is leaving the smell of tobacco all over their home in New Road, Eyam. 'We don't mind having a ghost,' explained Gordon. 'It worried us at first but you soon get used to it. He isn't any trouble and we would hardly notice him if it wasn't for his pipe smoking.. Neither of us smoke, so it is a bit annoying when you get the smell of pipe tobacco all over the house. You never actually see the smoke but the smell is unmistakable.'
>
> The ghost was first noticed in the Robinson's home several years ago when pictures started to move mysteriously and a glass chandelier hanging in the living room was found lying on the floor, totally undamaged.
>
> 'We couldn't understand it at first,' said Gordon, 'but when it became obvious that something was moving things, we were finally convinced we had a resident ghost.' They often hear the sound of someone pacing round their home, and according to Hannah, their home is not the only one on the estate that has experienced ghostly goings on. 'I have heard one or two people talk about ornaments or decorations being moved to different places of the house,' she said. 'It seems very strange because although this is a very old village, the houses on this estate are only just over 50 years old. (1960 build)
>
> The popular idea that ghosts only haunt old properties is quite untrue, they are just as likely to haunt a new build, because it is now recognised that residual energy does not necessarily exist in only the fabric of a building. It can hang around in the ether or emanate from the ground oblivious to any building that has been erected since the unquiet spirit passed over.

Turn right at the junction and at the end of the road is Church Street. Opposite are the gates of Eyam Hall Craft Centre. Turn left and proceed back to Hawkhill Road and the car park which is the start/end of this walk.

4: Bretton & Bretton Clough

THE PHANTOM HUNT & THE GABRIEL HOUNDS

5 miles (8·10km)

This walk begins at the Hawkhill car park in Eyam, but if you prefer a shorter walk – 3½ miles (5·65km), you can begin at The Barrel Inn in Bretton. Park in the pub car park or on the road if this is full, or you are not using the other facilities of this ancient hostelry.

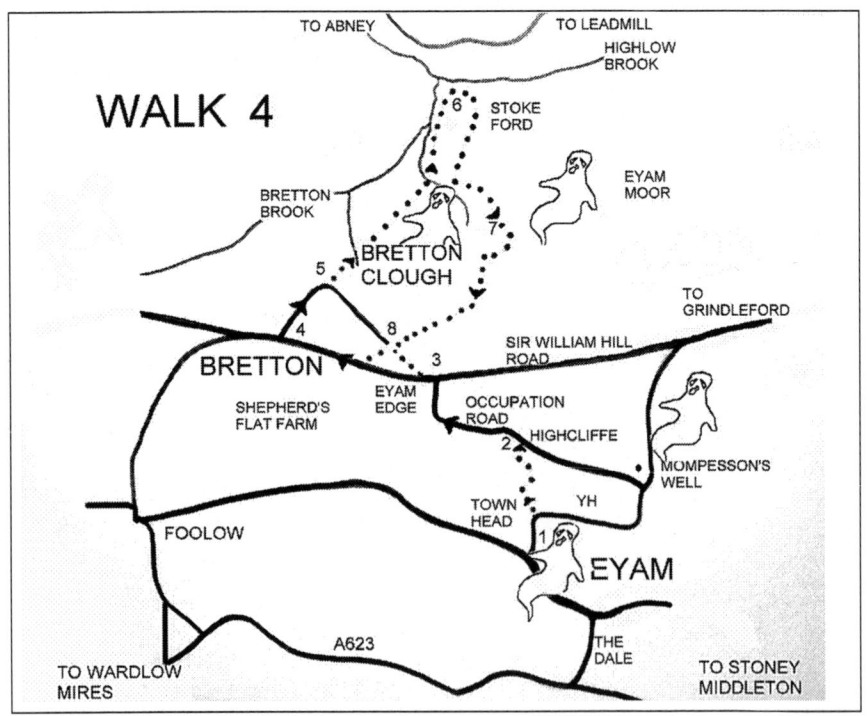

The Walk

Leave Hawkhill car park by the entrance – 1. Turn right and walk up Hawkhill Road. Continue up the hill heading north, and where Hawkhill Road veers to the right, turn left onto the lane, an old bridle way that becomes a rough track climbing steadily for ½ mile.

Eyam was once a hive of industrial activity as this old photograph shows but there were still periods of unemployment

On reaching the road this is an area called Highcliffe – 2 and the road is named Occupation Road, because it was built around 1790 to provide employment during a period of industrial recession.

It was during this time that an ancient, richly decorated cinerary urn, used for storing the ashes of the dead after cremation, was found by Mr S Furness of Eyam. This is just one indication that this area was inhabited by prehistoric man, something that we will encounter repeatedly on this walk.

Turn left and follow the road for about half a mile until reaching the end of Sir William Hill Road – 3 – a one time pack horse route and salt road linking Sheffield with Buxton. At one point is rises above 1,400 ft. There is a short stretch evocative of the 18th century turnpike which is what it was, as a turnpike road was constructed in 1757 as part of the route between Sheffield, Buxton and Manchester.

It's uncertain which William they were honouring when naming the road. It could have been Sir William Peveril, powerful Norman baron and builder of Peveril Castle, or William Cavendish, Bess of Hardwick's grandson of nearby Chatsworth House, or William Saville, Lord of the Manor of Eyam.

In 1912, a cinerary urn, was found near the verge of Sir William Hill and in great need of restoration, is in the church vestry. The story of its find is in the 1912 edition of the *Derbyshire Archaeological Journal*.

Andrew Merrill who lived at Hollins House survived the plague by coming to the summit of Sir William Hill Road and building a crude hut in which he lived with his pet cockerel until the plague was over.

Apparently, one morning after strutting around for a while, the cock flapped his wings and flew back to its old home. Merrill pondered for a day or two over the meaning of his companion's abrupt departure, then decided that just as Noah had sent the dove to see whether the waters had subsided after the flood, the bird's departure could signify the end of the plague. Andrew Merrill collected up his belongings and returned to Eyam to find the cockerel on his old perch and the plague had abated. He and his pet cockerel had escaped the plague.

Turn left and take the miner road towards Bretton perched conspicuously upon the spine of Hucklow Edge.

Just before reaching Bretton, note the footpath on the left which takes you to Shepherd's Flat Farm, now a substantial building of Georgian design. At the rear of the house are farm buildings, fragments of which appear to have survived from the 17th century, because built into a corner of one of these can be seen two stones roughly carved with several letters, one of which has been obliterated by a smudge of cement. These stones were lettered by Matthew Mortin as a memorial to his wife and children who died in the plague. At the time of the plague there were two houses in this area; the Mortins lived at what is now Shepherd Flat Farm and at a neighbouring cottage lived a widow named Lydia Kempe with her four children. As a result of these children playing with children from Eyam, the plague was brought to this lonely spot where on July 13th Robert Kempe died. His sister Elizabeth died on August 11th, followed by his brothers Thomas and Michael on the 12th and 15th. A week later Lydia Kempe was buried with her children.

The Mortins must have been horrified because Mrs Mortin was in the advance stages of pregnancy and as the time of birth drew near, Mr Matthew Mortin went down into Eyam to obtain the services of the village mid-wife. Despite his ardent appeals, the woman adamantly refused her services. Returning to his home, Matthew Morton found his eldest son Robert aged three screaming in agony; he had contracted the plague. Within a few days Robert and his two year old sister Sarah were dead, closely followed by Mrs Mortin and her newborn son. Matthew buried his little family and recorded this sad event on the gable end of the shippen, once the old house – He carved the initials of his older children and a small 's' for the tiny son who died unbaptised.

Bretton – 4 is a tiny, bleak hamlet with a pub and a few farmsteads. Those taking the shorter route will join the walk here.

The Barrel Inn at Bretton dates back to 1597 and once served travellers on the Sir William Hill Road during and prior to its turnpike days. It stands 1,300ft above sea level and claims to be the highest pub in Derbyshire, and the third highest in England, offering views over five counties.

The tiny hamlet of Bretton with the Barrel Inn at the heart

There's further evidence that this area was inhabited by prehistoric man when more cinerary urns were found at Bretton. They are now in Western Park Museum, Sheffield.

Flax was grown on fields behind the Barrel Inn, and flax spinning would have been a local cottage industry for the women and children. Most of the men would have been employed in the lead mines which gives us a perplexing story. Apparently the miners ran a burial club at The Barrel Inn, but it had one unusual rule; a member had to give two weeks notice of death or the money would not be paid. As no one ever made a claim, the miners disposed of the fund by having a party at The Barrel Inn every Christmas.

Take the narrow road to the left of The Barrel Inn and one of the farmsteads that now serves as a Youth Hostel.

Even though the isolated hamlet of Bretton is 1½ miles from Eyam, it was still affected by the plague. At Bretton Youth Hostel you'll find several dressed stones lying in careless confusion, examine them for traces of inscriptions. Just above the water course among the unkempt grass beneath the wall are a row of five sunken stones to perpetuate the sad event. One bore the initials P.M indicating the grave of Peter Mortin, the first plague victim who died at Bretton on February 4th 1666. Six months later on the last day of July, Ann Mortin died. Sarah Blackwell died on August 13th; Peter Hall on August 23rd and Ann Townsend on September 22nd.

Leaving the Youth Hostel, the road descends gently for about ¼ mile. Where the road bends to the right – 5, keep straight forward here, following the guide posted footpath between walls. Cross a stile and descend the easy, green path, going towards Bretton Clough, a delightful valley with trickling streams and steep hillsides cloaked in ancient woodland. By a second seat, turn sharp right with the path, descending more steeply now over stonier, wetter ground. After crossing the narrow stream feeding into Bretton Brook – 6 a stretch of more open ground follows.

The narrow clapper bridge crossing the stream at Bretton Clough

Where the path branches, keep straight ahead, below and to the left of a ruined farmstead, and re-enter Bretton Clough, but watch out!

Bretton Clough is a secluded wooded valley that has an eerie reputation in the neighbouring villages. The name is of ancient Celtic origin meaning 'the farm of the Britons', and it's said to be haunted by a phantom huntsman and hounds. In The Ghost Book, A.A Mc Gregor writes that among the people who claim to have seen the phantom hunt were the Rev. Brooksbank, a former vicar of Hathersage church, and the Hodgkinson sisters, owners of Moorseats Hall.

Spectral hounds are often heard but seldom seen at Bretton Clough

Dr Mary Andrews of Shatton, the author of Long Ago in Peakland, also reports that during the 1930s she and a companion were walking through Bretton Clough when they heard the sound of a hunting horn. They looked around expecting to see a hunt approaching but there was nothing and they could find no explanation for the sound of the horn. It was some years later that she heard for the first time about the phantom hunt often heard in the valley.

> Belief in the phantom hunt is very ancient and widespread. It could have Viking origin. One of their myths was the legend of the Hounds of Odin, also known as the Hounds of the Underworld or Otherworld – the regions below the earth's surface – the abode of the dead. It could stem from ancient Greek mythology and the goddess Diana who on a white horse and accompanied by her pack of spectral hounds rides across the moonlit sky searching for lost souls.

Descend to the hidden beauty spot of Stoke Ford – 6 – a popular picnic spot for generations of ramblers. There's a little footbridge over the Bretton Brook which goes on to join Highlow Brook, and here at the confluence three cloughs meet; Bretton, Highlow and Abney. This is where *Walks 3 and 4* meet and share the next ghostly story.

> Throughout England, there are tales of spectral hounds that howl as they glide through the sky on wild, stormy nights. Often they are heard rather than seen and the sound of their ghostly cries are said to be a sign of impending death or doom. In North Derbyshire and the Peak District they are known as The Rach Hounds or Gabriel Hounds. A rational explanation would be that the sound is made by geese but people who have heard them are unconvinced. The prophetic ability of these hounds was widely accepted, and at the outbreak of the plague in Eyam, many of the people were sure that they had previously heard the Gabriel Hounds. There's also a romantic story in Derbyshire of how this widespread belief served a useful purpose in thwarting the intentions of an unacceptable suitor.
>
> The Bowman family lived at the bottom of this lonely dell in the 1800's and eighteen year old Mary had attracted the attention of a young man called Birch whose parents cultivated a small farm in the area. They had fallen in love and in due course hoped to marry but Mary's father was against the idea, believing that his daughter would be marrying beneath herself.
>
> It was during this time that a gentleman called Galliard arrived on the scene to partake of two week's shooting on Eyam Moor, and arrangements were made for him to stay with the Bowmans. Unsurprisingly, he began to show a great interest in Mary and decided to woo her. In her father's eyes, Galliard was a much more acceptable suitor for his daughter than the lowly Birch so he did everything in his power to encourage the young man despite the fact that Mary was unresponsive. Unable to go against her father's wishes, Mary and Birch decided that

drastic action was needed and with the help of Mary's brother they devised a plan.

Mary suddenly fell ill and was confined to bed, but instead of getting better, she grew worse. No one knew what was wrong but everyone stood in shocked silence when the distant sound of the spectral hounds was heard. The howling increased as the hounds approached the Bowman's house until the sound was no more than a single dog panting as it settled outside. Having signalled Mary's death, the sound moved swiftly away and disappeared in the distance. Her shocked parents now knew that Mary only had a short time to live. Galliard, who was visiting Mary at the time also understood the significance of this event, and fearing that the illness might be infectious, made a hasty departure from Derbyshire.

After Mr Bowman had bid his guest a rather regretful farewell, he returned to the house to be told by his wife – 'She is gone my Mary!'

Mr Bowman obviously assumed the worse, but in actual fact, as soon as Galliard had left, Mary had leapt out of her bed to meet Birch and her brother at a pre-arranged rendezvous where the plotters, who had impersonated the spectral hounds so convincingly, could congratulate themselves on a job well-done.

The views across the valley are remarkable

Retrace your steps for a short distance only, soon branching left with the path to climb steeply out of the Clough. The gradient eases a little as the path veers right, but if you pause and look around, the views are remarkable.

It's rather a tedious climb back out of the valley, but continue along a green track beside the wall, bending left over a side valley and still climbing.

Cross a stile and continue, still following the wall to Gotherage Plantation – 7. Bear right over a step-stile and continue, still by the wall side on a green track that feeds into a farm track. When you arrive at a crossways – 8, our paths

Another view across the valley

divide. If your starting point was Bretton, cross the stile and continue ahead along a rough lane until reaching the road. Turn right and walk back to The Barrel. If your starting point was Eyam, after crossing the stile, branch left until reaching the road – 3, then retrace your steps back to Eyam.

5: Highcliffe – Stanage – Abney – Highlow – Leam – Eyam Moor – Wet Withens – Sir William Hill Road – Mompesson's Well – Eyam Churchyard

The Phantom & the Carter – Haunted Highlow Hall – Lost Love – Phantom Coach – Ghost Lights & Malevolent Spirits

7 miles (11·35km)

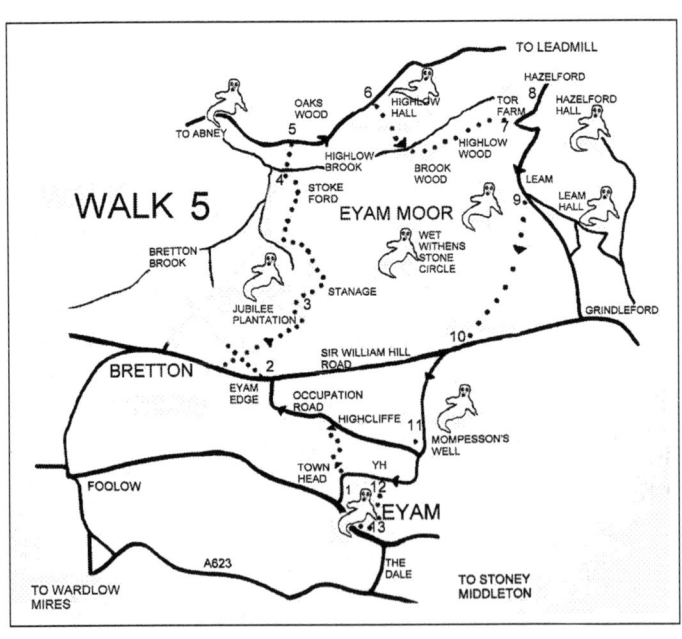

The Walk
This walk begins at Hawkhill car park – 1 and takes the same route as *Walk 4*, going up Hawkhill Road, turning left to climb up the old bridle way to Highcliffe, then left to Sir William Hill Road. From the point where the road turns left to Bretton, go 75 metres, then leave the road to take a gravel track on the right – 2. (*Walk 4* continues into Bretton, but the routes cross again at Stoke Ford).

Follow this track for about 275 metres and at a cross road of tracks, turn right over the ladder stile signed Stoke Ford.

Follow a wide path with a wall on your left passing rhododendrons and Jubilee Plantation – 3. After passing a small, low building, leave the wall on the left to continue uphill to the top corner of a wood and stone gate posts. The farmhouse over on your right derives its name Stanage from the site on which it was erected near an enormous stone tumuli. Plundered and destroyed over the centuries, as so often happened the stone was used for buildings and walls.

Continue ahead along a wide, grass path to cross a stile by a gate. Keep straight on following the wall close on your left and going round a right hand bend. Cross a stile by a gate and turn left.

Continue to follow the wall and woodland then moorland on your left with the western edge of Eyam Moor up on your right. Cross a stile by a gate in the moorland corner and follow the wide grass path along the ridge.

Cross one stile and follow the path as it veers away from the wall on your right and descend to Stoke Ford – 4, a popular picnic spot for generations of ramblers. Aim for the little footbridge over the Bretton Brook which goes on to join Highlow Brook. Here three cloughs meet; Bretton, Highlow and Abney. This is where *Walk 4 and 5* meet up and share a ghostly story which you can read in *Walk 4*

Cross the bridge and after 300 metres the footpath comes out on the lane between Abney and Leadmill – 5.

Bretton Clough

A Carter in his horse drawn trap made a regular journey along the lonely lane from Leadmill to Abney and on various occasions, a phantom figure would appear and take the horse's bridle to lead it for a short way. This did not unduly disturb the carter or spook his horse, but the carter's dog would lie cowering in the trap, its hair bristling with fear. One day however when the phantom appeared, the driver was caught unawares and involuntarily raised his whip. Instantly his arm fell to his side limp and useless and he never recovered from his paralysis.

The lane between Abney and Highlow where a phantom figure took the horse's reins

Turn right and walk about 600 m along the lane towards Leadmill, but watch out for that phantom! Ahead of you on the right of the road overlooking Hathersage is the ancient Highlow Hall, a battlemented manor house now a farm, with a quaint ball-topped gateway and a stone dovecote – 6.

Highlow is a name that seems to contradict itself yet 'low' is actually derived from the Old English word 'hlaw' meaning hill and was usually given to a place where ancient chambered tombs, stone circles and burial mounds have been found. In Derbyshire many of the place names that end on Low occur on leylines.

Highlow Hall, once said to be the most haunted house in Derbyshire

Once labelled the most haunted house in Derbyshire, the story of Highlow Hall goes back to the days of 1340 when Nicholas Eyre, eldest son of the Lord of the Manor of Hope was a frequent visitor. The cad was having a relationship with both the Archer sisters, the co-heiresses of the property. Not surprisingly when the eldest daughter caught him at his little game, she was not too pleased and what happened next we can only surmise because she disappeared from Highlow in circumstances unknown.

The two timing Nicholas Eyre married the younger daughter and would have lived happily ever after if her sister hadn't appeared as a ghost. This must have been rather awkward because she not only blamed Nicholas for her death, she apparently turned to face him and declared that she had put a curse on the family. They would marry into the best families and prosper to the fifteenth generation, then loose everything. Over the following generations, everything the ghost predicted came true and by 1842 their fortunes had gone, their extensive acres had dwindled and various branches of the family became extinct.

But did the disappearance of the jilted sister have any connection with the bumps and bangs that are heard from time to time on the stair treads? Legend says yes! They are said to be the phantom echoes of an incident when a lady was murdered in one of the upstairs rooms and her body dragged along the landing and down the stairs to be buried in an unmarked grave.

Heralded by a rustling of silk skirts, a ghostly white lady was often seen crossing the old courtyard to enter the front door and ascend the oak staircase. A farm-worker who saw the phantom several times by moonlight found her so life-like, he was in the habit of touching his cap and making a formal greeting, yet there was never any reply or hint of recognition. She has also been seen standing with the palms of her hands resting on the edge of a cattle trough, gazing into the water and no doubt contemplating her own reflection while wondering why Nicholas Eyre jilted her in favour of her sister.

Take the footpath on your right just before Highlow Hall. After 500m the footpath crosses Highlow Brook. Continue straight ahead into Brook Wood, an established conifer and silver birch wood.

Cross a stile and continue in the same direction crossing three fields and going through three gateways.

At Tor Farm – 7, go through two gates then bear slightly right up the farm drive to reach the road at Hazelford – 8.

During the time of the plague, bread was brought from Hazelford by a man called Cooper and was left upon a certain boulder near the Druid's Circle. Another person is said to have brought victuals from Little Common, then a hamlet near Sheffield and left them there too.

These designated drop off points are to be found in many parts of the country and are known as 'plague stones', 'leper stones' or 'penny stones'. It is not unlikely that Pennistone near Sheffield obtained its name from the existence of such a stone.

Bernard Wells of Hazelford Hall fell in love with Anne Moreton, the niece of one of his father's tenants who lived at a farmhouse on the edge of the River Derwent. When the father, also named Bernard realised that his son intended to marry the girl, he ordered her uncle to stop the liaison or be evicted from his property and having no wish to be evicted from his home and livelihood, Mr Moreton tried to reason with the lovesick girl who had been placed in his charge after the death of her father on May 23rd 1646.

In the meanwhile at Hazelford Hall, Mr Wells was making arrangements for his son to go away for ten months, a prospect which Bernard found unacceptable. Despite all his pleas, his father was adamant, so Bernard decided that the only course open to them was to elope.

That evening after Anne had retired to bed, she was startled by a gentle rap on the lattice window and the voice of Bernard Wells urging her to dress quickly. Trembling with agitation, she dressed and joined her lover outside. He quickly outlined his plan and without a moments hesitation, Anne agreed to leave with him that night despite the darkness and the rain which beat down in torrents. Soon they reached the banks of the Derwent which they could hear rather than see in the sheer blackness. Their plan was to cross the stepping stones above Leadmill Bridge and make their way to Peak Forest where they could be married in the church, but the river was fast and dangerous and scarcely had they started to cross when Bernard lost his footing and they both fell into the icy water. Bernard struggled to make it to the opposite bank, but Anne was washed away downstream.

Bernard's tormented cries roused the neighbourhood, yet despite a search they couldn't find Anne. Next morning the search was resumed but to no avail. Days were spent searching for her body but it was never found. Bernard Wells wandered unceasingly along the banks of the Derwent month after month, year after year until he died a melancholy death calling her name in his last breath. He was laid to rest in Eyam church, but his ghost is said to continue his lonely vigil wandering along the banks of the River Derwent called the name of his lost love.

> The years passed and almost a century later a fisherman discovered the fleshless arm of a female in the Derwent. It was put in a box which was placed on the windowsill in the north-west aisle of Eyam church. There it remained for a great number of years, an object of curiosity linked with this poem entitled the Maid of Derwent
>
> The night was dark and sheets of rain came sweeping from the skies,
> When Anne held her fevered brain and breathed a thousand sighs.
> A lone and latticed window nigh, upon her bed she lay
> Weeping her fate, when suddenly a voice it seemed to say
> My Love, my life, awake, arise Beneath the shades of night
> We must away or ah! Mine eyes no more shall see the light
> Twas her beloved Wells and to his arms, she wond'ring, trembling went
> Her fluttering heart beat with alarms, her head she slowly bent.
> A moment passed then forth they paced to Derwent's sable flood
> Through darkness deep, they sped in haste, till on the bank they stood
> To cross the mountain headlong stream they stepped from stone to stone
> They slipped alas and then a scream, waked darkness on her throne!
> Into the flood sweet Anne sank- deaths pangs ah! Soon were o'er
> To her the past became a blank, a vision now no more.
> Wells struggled, reached the stones again – his voice now rose above
> In cries – in lamentations vain, for his fond perished love.
> Now milkmaids fondly, plaintive sing, beneath the mountain shade,
> Till vales and woods echoing ring of Derwent's hapless maid.

Either turn left and walk into Leadmill where refreshment can be obtained at The Plough Inn, or turn right and walk along the road for nearly ¼ mile passing Leam Farm and Cottage. At the branch road by the second farm – 9, take the footpath on the right. A slight detour to your left would take you to Leam Hall and our next ghost story.

> Prior to 1939 when Leam Hall became part of the Youth Hostel Association, it was a private mansion of considerable charm. It reverted back to a private residence in the mid 1950's although this story dates from the earlier period when admittance to the courtyard was by a pair of large white gates which were kept closed at all times. This meant that they had to be opened and closed immediately before and after the entrance or exit of any person or vehicle.
>
> One evening, the groom and his boy assistant left the stables to meet what they believed to be the family carriage returning home. Both could

hear the distinct sound of galloping horses and as the sound came nearer they waited at the entrance in readiness to open the gates for the coach bearing their returning master and mistress. But instead of the familiar carriage, a strange carriage and pair appeared round the bend of the drive, galloped towards them and disappeared through the closed white gates. The two men stared in shocked disbelief because the coachman had no head.

Cross the stile onto Eyam Moor to follow the well defined path. The moor which is crowned by Sir William Hill, 1418ft above sea level is rich in chambered tombs, stone circles and burial mounds, the littered reminders of our Bronze Age ancestors. In the Bronze Age period, this area would have been covered with rich farm land and woodland, not the dry peat moors of today.

Eyam Moor was home to our Bronze Age ancestors

Farming communities would have been dotted around the area and intermingled with the round houses where extended families would live together, would have been the burial mounds now recognisable as low hummocks in the heather.

Most of the lumps and bumps have now been investigated but there could be more. Many have been badly plundered although according to scanty records, they never held anything more than a few personal objects and cinerary urns containing the ashes of the long dead. Around the end of the 18th century, Joseph Slinn and William Redfern were working near Bolehill, on Eyam Moor when they discovered an urn, and although Slinn wanted to secure it intact, Redfern smashed it to pieces to see whether it contained treasure. It contained ashes and two Roman coins.

There is much evidence of primitive man's passing around Eyam Moor. On what is called Smith's Piece, there is an enormous gritstone rock, containing a rock basin marked on ordnance survey maps – 218. 783 Whether it was hollowed out by the natural action of rain water or the

Eyam Moor

work of man is unsure, but it was allegedly a place of pilgrimage where thousands of years ago people placed votive offerings. It could also have acted as a trading place during the plague, the basin holding water or vinegar to clean the coins.

The site of another large tumulus was on land called Hawley's Piece. An urn of great size and antiquity was discovered near the centre and the finder took it home with him. When the superstitious finder lost a young cow and began to experience a period of bad luck, he decided that the precious relic was unlucky and buried it.

Almost in the centre of Eyam Moor is a large embanked stone circle known as Wet Withens, one of the county's least visited pre-historic sites. Out in the open moor it is hard to locate, but it is marked on ordnance survey maps at 226.790, and by popular tradition, it is said to have been the centre of Druid ritual and ceremony.

> *This stone circle was known to have been used like a market place during the period of the plague. Market people, having their mouths primed with*

tobacco which they believed was a preservative, brought their provisions then stood at a distance from the people with whom they were going to traffic. The buyers were not able to touch any of the articles before purchase, but when the agreement was finished, they would take the goods and deposit the money in the shallow waters of the stream that passes close by.

Wet Withens now consists of ten obvious standing stones set in a bank of approximately 30m in diameter. Most of the stones lean at quite an angle, but when upright, all would have been under 1 metre tall. A drawing from the 1800's shows 16 stones. In the 1842 book *The History and Antiquities of Eyam* – William Wood refers to this as an Ortholitic Circle, a stone circle of about 100ft in diameter with 12 – 16 standing stones. Ignoring the discrepancy in the number of stones, we can't ignore the fact that this was a very special place. For many hundreds of years, people would have travelled here from miles around to worship their gods and ask for help with the harvest or to ensure the continued fertility of the land and community.

One of the stones on Eyam Moor

Stone circles are thought to have been a special place where chieftains and important people were buried in the belief that the power contained within its stones would transport their souls to the afterlife

It is still believed that these stones have special powers. They can help healing, aid conception, and hold electrical energy. Some people who touch the stones are able to feel the energy and there are even claims that it is possible to get a mild electric shock. People who are particularly sensitive to changes in atmospheric pressure have reported hearing faint sounds like whining, humming or buzzing much like those

> emitted from transformers and power lines coming from the stones. It has also been claimed that these unusual energies can be seen like a transparent heat haze that sprays into the air before dispersing and disappearing. At its most powerful, this energy leaks out into the atmosphere creating visual changes in the air which causes particles to be charged and transformed into ghostly balls of light.

> Over the centuries there have been continuous reports of strange lights in and around Eyam Moor. They form part of the local folklore. A strange glow in 1600 would have been considered a ghost light of demonic origin; in 2000 it would be reported as a UFO, so explanations have changed but the lights remain.
>
> Ghostly lights are often said to hover over old standing stones and with a name like Wet Withens these sightings are readily explained – marsh gases. The rotting vegetation and animal matter produces a chemical soup that bubbles up through the bog letting off unctuous, condensed vapours. But what ignites these gases and wouldn't the vapours be more likely to burn on the surface rather than float upwards and hover as if caught and carried by air currents?
>
> Our ancestors believed that mischievous fairies or evil spirits used lights to lead mesmerised travellers from their safe paths to bogs, mires and pools where they would be swallowed up. It's the stuff of fairytales, but what better theories do we have – so watch out?
>
> Some say the moor is haunted by many malevolent spirits and on moonlit nights the area is filled with the sound of weeping and wailing. For centuries, people have been experiencing strange occurrences and ghostly sightings at the stone circle. Folk memory, rumours and anecdotes of boggarts and spectral black dogs have been augmented by the claims of psychics. There is certainly an atmosphere about the place and it is not difficult to see why an ancient site like this has long been regarded as a place of power where unusual forces can manifest. This quiet, isolated places, has a strange mystical quality that owes much to its long forgotten past.

The Romans would have tramped across this moor and the pack horses carrying the areas most precious commodity – lead.

A conical block of lead was found on Eyam Moor many years ago. It was probably jolted off a wagon or pack-horse carrying pigs of lead or ingots. It weighed 30lb and had a hook or handle attached, probably to disengage it from the mould or to facilitate its easier handling.

If you have not been tempted to stray from the footpath, after about ¾ miles, you reach a fence on your left. Follow this fence for about ¼ mile until reaching a roadside gate – 10. Cross the stile onto the road at the junction of Sir William Hill Road. Bear slightly right, then cross the road to walk down Edge Road towards Eyam. After about ¼ mile you will pass Mompessons Well – 11 and the Bretton road on your right. Continue down Edge Road, passing Hollowbrook Barn and ignoring the woodland path to continue down the road until reaching the  Youth Hostel on your right. Go through a small gate opposite on your left into a field – 12. Keep to the path on your right and follow it down as it becomes steps. Go through a small gate at the bottom of the steps and turn left. Carry on down with the wall on your left until at the bottom of the field you will see gate posts ahead and a stile to the right. Cross through the stile and follow the lane down to the graveyard which you enter through a gate – 13. See *Walk 1* for stories of the haunted graveyard and village. Walk through the churchyard then exit onto Church Street. Turn right and follow the road back to the car-park which is the start/end of this walk.

6: Riley Graves – Stoney Middleton – Boundary Stone – Lydgate Graves

THE GHOST AT THE GRAVES – PHANTOM FIGURE
OF FLORA – SPECTRE CROSSING – STRANGE SMELLS
AT THE HALL – RED RETURNS

3¼ miles (5·25km)

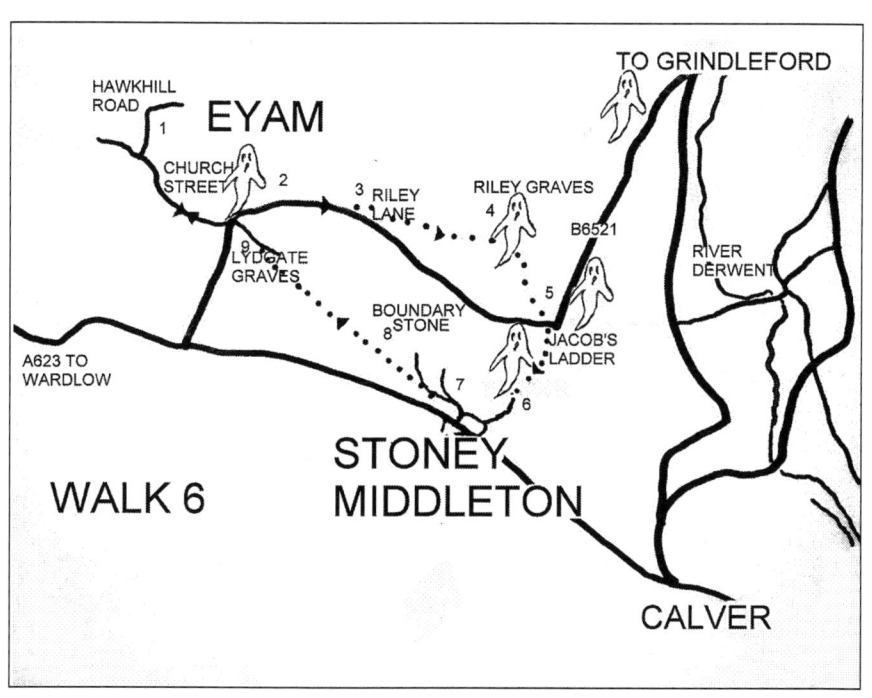

The Walk

Leave the Hawkhill car park – 1 by the entrance and turn left down Hawkhill Road. At the T junction, turn left into Church Street. Follow it through the village to The Square then up The Causeway – B6521 – passing the Wesleyan Reform Chapel on your right and Riley Back Lane on your left – 2. Walk past these and the two rows of cottages know as Burch Row and Burch Place, and continue up the hill which becomes New Road. Shortly, the road forks, so take the left hand branch into Riley Lane – 3, guide posted to Riley Graves.

Take the left branch into Riley Lane

Riley is an area and the name comes from Rois Leys which means King's field. William Wood refers to the former existence of several large stones which formed a prehistoric circle near Riley and when taking up the foundations of an old wall here in the late 18th century, Robert Broomhead of Eyam broke an ancient burial urn. As we have seen in other walks, these are not just isolated finds, many ancient tumuli and their contents, mainly cinerary urns have been found at various times around Eyam. Perhaps there are still more to find

Follow Riley Lane on a gentle climb uphill for about 360m until you come to a fork. Bear right and continue up the lane for approximately 280m where you will see the wall surrounding the Riley Graves – 4 in a field on your left about ¼ mile outside the village.

The Riley graves are surrounded by a protective wall

About 50 yards from the enclosed cemetery is an ash tree standing in a North-east direction of the stones. A few yards south of this tree was the home of the Hancocks although nothing now remains. The family consisted of John Hancock, his wife and six children.

About 250 yards west or rather north-west of the Hancock home was the home of the Talbot family which consisted of Richard Talbot, his wife Catherine, three sons (although one had left home) and three daughters. The present Riley Farmhouse is built on its site. Richard Talbot was a blacksmith and had a smithy adjoining the house, and close to the road because in those early days, the road from Manchester to Sheffield passed close by this property.

The pestilence had raged ten months in Eyam when on July 5th 1666 the plague arrived at Riley with the death of Bridget and Mary Talbot. Two days later, Ann the third daughter died. The mother Catherine died on July 18th followed by son Robert on the 24th. The following day the father Richard died leaving only one son who died on July 30th They were all buried hurriedly without any form of religious ceremony, interred together close by their home and in the orchard of the present Riley House. The monument with the inscription 'Richard Talbot, Catherine his wife, two sons and three daughters, buried July 1666' is almost erased.

The last of the Talbots was probably buried by their neighbours the Hancocks, and thus the plague passed to them. On August 3rd, only three days later, two of the children John and Elizabeth Hancock both died and were buried a short distance from their home. On August 6th son Oner died, followed by husband John and son William – three deaths in one day. Alice died on August 9th and Ann on the 10th and according to tradition, Mrs Hancock buried them all single handedly, then left to live with her only surviving son who was an apprentice in Sheffield. It was this son who erected the tomb and stones in memory of his family, but the site of the graves was on the common or moor. When this was later enclosed, in order to preserve what would have been forgotten graves, Thomas Birds, an Eyam antiquary had the stones removed, and the inscriptions incised more deeply. They were then placed closer together and surrounded by a stone wall, and now this enclosure is perhaps the most visited of the plague memorials.

The headstone of John Hancock is possibly in its original place and bears the inscription –

'Remember man, As though goest by,
As though art now, even so was I

As I do now, so must thou lye
Remember Man, that thou shalt die

On the six headstones that have been brought together the inscriptions are –

Elizabeth Hancock, Buried Aug 3 1666
John Hancock, Buried Aug 3 1666
Oner Hancock, Buried Aug 7 1666
William Hancock, Buried Aug 7 1666
Alice Hancock, Buried Aug 9 1666
Ann Hancock, Buried Aug 10 1666

The site, high on the hillside above Eyam, is now ringed by a protective heart shaped stone wall, and it is possible to visit these graves, but don't be surprised if you encounter Mrs Hancock. She was the only surviving member of the family and is probably still visiting their graves, because a woman in a blue dress is said to haunt the Riley Graves. She moves amongst the graves as if tending them but as you get nearer, she simply melts away.

Does Mrs Hancock still haunt the Riley graves

Leaving the site, continue uphill and at a private road turn right onto a path into a wooded area. At the next junction turn right and follow the path down the hill. When you reach a gate, go through it and continue straight on with the wall on your left. To your left are impressive views of Froggatt, Curbar and Baslow Edge. Where the track meets the B6521 road from Eyam to Grindleford, go through a stile at the side of a gate – 5.

Go through a stile at the side of the gate

A beautiful young woman is said to wander round here. More than once I've heard her referred to as Fair Flora which is quite a coincidence because a classical statue of Flora, the Greek goddess of flowers is ¾ mile (1·20km) down this road hidden away in a small plantation at Goatscliffe.

There are various stories woven around this statue and why she should be sited in such a remote place, but I prefer the sad ballad entitled *The Astrologer's Daughter* by J Castle Hall which links the statue with this story:-

A gypsy girl named Flora fell in love with Victor, the son of the local squire. They married and set up home together in a small cottage near Grindleford close to the woods where they had met, and for a time they were extremely happy, then Victor had to go away to war. Twelve months passed before Victor returned to find the cottage abandoned. He was mystified yet as he looked around, he saw his wife coming towards him. She was dressed in the purest white garments; her arms were outstretched but as he ran to embrace her, his arms passed through her outline as if it was a shadow. He had seen her ghost.

He later found that Flora had died giving birth to a baby daughter adopted by the gypsies, so in her memory Victor erected the statue of Flora on the site where they met. Her ghost is still said to haunt the area, and some say that when the moon is full, her statue comes alive

There are more stories related to this statue which we visit on *Walk 7*.

In the 1970's the father of a young Grindleford businessman told Clarence Daniels of his son's experience when driving along this road from Eyam to Grindleford. He had returned home shaken and upset, as on the journey he had seen an indistinct figure shrouded in cloak and hood, cross the road from the top of Jacob's Ladder, an old bridle-road climbing steeply from Stoney Middleton. At one time this would have been a major thoroughfare used as part of the daily grind for men and women who walked from out-lying hamlets around Grindleford to work in the boot and shoe factories at Stoney Middleton.

The man had stopped his car and watched the figure pass through the solid

A photograph dating from 1916 of Jacob's Ladder from where a ghostly apparition appeared

stone wall to proceed up the old cart-track in the direction of the disused Riley slate-pits. Shocked and dazed by the experience, he sat at the wheel some time before recovering enough composure the resume his journey.

Although many people think of ghosts as formless wraiths or insubstantial spirit images wreathed in a shroud-like astral attire, most ghosts have the appearance of physical solidity, clothed in garments which have a realistic quality; the type of attire worn by the phantoms during the days of their mortality.

From this point *Walk 7* continues to Stoke, Froggatt and Calver, but to continue *Walk 6* to Stoney Middleton, we will take that old route – Jacob's Ladder, so watch out! Cross the road and turn immediately left. Walk a few paces then turn sharp right, do not take the footpath by the gateway. This surfaced lane will take you down the hill with the two ponds on your left, but ignore the footpath by the ponds. Follow the lane down the hill, to arrive at The Nook – 6.

The Roman baths

On your right is the spring and the Roman Baths, a neat, single storey stone bath house restored between 1985/92. It is believed to have been built on the site of a Roman bath, and judging by the amount of Roman finds in the area, that is definitely a possibility.

Tradition insists that an elevated oval-shaped eminence called Castle Hill at Stoney Middleton was the site of a Roman encampment. Roman coins have been found in its vicinity and when pulling down a barn near to Castle Hill, an antique battle axe was found.

There was certainly a large Roman presence in the area, and we know that amongst other things, they introduced bathing for recreational, curative and cleaning purposes. Although the baths at Buxton are better known and were much frequented by the Romans who preferred the warmer waters, the spring water at Stoney Middleton were sought for the relief of rheumatism and such maladies as 'too great heat' and 'stillness of blood'.

In 1734 Dr Short's treatise on Mineral Waters claimed that the water could be drunk more freeely and safely than at Buxton as it is cooler. In 1789, a writer called Pilkington suggested that more people would try the waters if the then open bath was covered in, a suggestion that was taken up by Thomas Denham of Stoney Middleton Hall. Not only was the bath covered, by 1815 there were separate baths for men and women, each with its own window, changing room and fireplace, but sadly this attempt to establish Stoney Middleton as a spa failed and the building gradually fell into disrepair. The building was restored between 1985-1992, and although the spring that feeds the bath house still flows at a constant temperature of 63 degrees, and is decorated during Stoney Middleton's well-dressing, the Roman baths are sadly not open to the public, even for viewing.

The spring that feeds the baths is still flowing

And on the subject of baths – a rather unique piece of Stoney Middleton parish property is the parish bath which some former benefactor bequeathed to the village for the benefit of any householder who lacked such an amenity.

For those who have only ever passed through Stoney Middleton along the A623 Middleton Dale, this part around the church will come as a delightful surprise. It is unexpectedly cosy with its crooked ways and sudden turns. The cottages and colourful gardens are quite charming and there is a little brook on its way to the grounds of the old hall, the previous parsonage and former home of the Denmans the most famous being Lord Thomas Denman, Lord Chief Justice in 1832 and Baron Denman of Dovedale in 1834. He was renowned as one of the greatest reformers of the Victorian age, an upright judge, a man of high moral character and one of the most persistent advocates of the abolition of slavery. This distinguished man was legendary for looking at life squarely and honestly and there's a village tale that on one occasion, a tenant accosted his lordship in the street and rebuked him because of the dire state his cottage was in. He threatened to leave if the required repairs were not carried out forthwith and the great lawyer listened in silence.

Until then he had not been aware that the cottage was his property, but a subsequent examination confirmed the tenants claim and the fact that he had not paid rent for seven years. The tenant was supplied with a rent book and the repairs were carried out, but as Lord Denman later confided to the man, if he had continued to live in the cottage without paying rent for just a little longer, he could legally have claimed it as his own.

Lord Denman's sons rose to high positions, one an admiral, and another a judge, but there's always one eccentric in any family. Apparently his son Thomas Denman who succeeded him, lived to be 89 and had the strange hobby of breeding black pigs and taking them for rides in his carriage or as presents for his friends.

Stoney Middleton Hall – haunted by phantom smells

There is no record of any ghosts at Stoney Middleton Hall but there are a number of instances of phantom fragrances. People sleeping in a certain bedroom are affected by the strange, inexplicable smell of sulphur, yet there is no fire in or anywhere near the room. It was so strong and insufferable on one occasion when the daughter of the house and a friend slept in this room that not only did it wake them, they had to get up and open the window.

A much more pleasant aroma drifted into the dreams of some friends who were staying with the Jessops at the time when they owned the house. They were woken by the appetizing aroma of bacon frying, yet in the small hours of the night it wasn't a midnight snack or an early breakfast. Not only was no meal of any sort being cooked, the bedroom was so far from the kitchen, they were unlikely to have smelt anything if it was.

Continue along the road as it bears left round the church. Note the lych gate, the roofed gateway to a church where traditionally coffin bearers waited for the clergyman to arrive.

This charming street scene hasn't changed in over a hundred years

Tradition has it that a crusader returned to his native Stoney Middleton with leprosy but was cured by bathing in the thermal spring. In thanksgiving, he erected a nearby chapel dedicated to St Martin, patron saint of soldiers and cripples. The church of St Martin later replaced the chapel, retaining the tower of an earlier edifice said to have been built by Joan Eyre in thanksgiving for the safe return of her husband from the 1415 Battle of Agincourt. When the main body of the church was re-built in 1759, it was given an unusual octagonal nave and chapel, and the octagonal theme is also echoed in the shape of its stone font and the pattern of central floor tiles.

The octagonal nave and chapel

There's a rather charming old custom that following a wedding at Stoney Middleton Church, a rope is fastened across the road along which the newly married couple will pass. In earlier times, on reaching the rope, the villagers would pelt them with sods of earth, old shoes and rice. It must have been quite messy and painful, but it was believed that the sods denoted plentiful produce from the ground, shoes meant good luck and rice meant plenty of children.

From at least the 16th century to the middle of the 20th, a standard way of wishing someone good luck on a journey or for a new undertaking was to throw an old shoe after them. *'For good luck, cast an olde shoe after mee,'* said a 1546 proverb.

From the 1820's, shoe-throwing was increasingly described as a wedding custom. For good luck, it was usual to fling a shoe after the bridal conveyance, or in the wake of the newly weds if they were obliged to trudge along on foot. At the sight of a wedding party, children would call out 'A wedding a woo, a clog and a shoe,' and pretend to take off their shoes and throw them at or after the couple. It was probably the number of direct hits that changed the custom from throwing to attaching to a wedding carriage.

But to continue our walk. Keep following the road, ignoring the road on your left which leads to the A623. Follow the minor road as it bears right then at the junction of The Fold and Cliff Bottom – 7, take the latter and walk up the hill.

> Several years ago, a family moved into a house at Stoney Middleton. The house suited them perfectly but there was one thing that left them rather perplexed. They often saw movement behind the floor length curtains as if a dog was passing by, then they saw a dog with a wavy red coat standing at the top of the stairs. They knew the name of the previous owner and after a bit of detective work were able to contact his sister who confirmed that while living there, her brother had in fact had a red-setter named Red.

Stoney Middleton has been described as stony by name, stony by nature, a true description when you contemplate the rugged, weather-beaten crags that project upwards like turrets and buttresses, in places three to four hundred feet high. A little way up Cliff Bottom, it is possible to look down on Middleton Dale and the A623 hemmed in by these looming crags, and of specific interest is the toll bar down below.

With the introduction of turnpike trusts from 1706, road tolls were levied at tollbars or turnpikes, their keepers often housed in adjoining rent-free cottages with distinctive collection windows or doorways facing in different directions. This rather unusual toll house constructed in 1840 is octagonal, and was built of gritstone with a slate roof, at a cost of £87.15. It was for occupation as a toll house on the Chesterfield/ Hernstone Lane Head turnpike, because Stoney Middleton was situated on an important coaching route. The 'Lucy Long' operated daily between Sheffield and Buxton during the summer season, and another coach ran to Sheffield every Tuesday, Thursday and Saturday and a Sheffield omnibus visited the village every Sunday. Lord Denman recorded in his diary that the miserable journey from Stoney Middleton to Buxton took three hours because of the steepness of the hills. You no longer have to stop here to pay a toll but as it's now a very popular fish and chip shop, it's still worth stopping.

Middleton Dale, hemmed in by looming crags

The Toll Bar Cottage

Another point of interest here is Lover's Leap. The name was kept alive by the Lovers Leap Café, once Lovers Leap Inn, built into the naked rocks that beetle over the property beside the A623 and recently changed.

The story goes back to around 1762 when Hannah Baddalay, daughter of William and Joan Baddalay, lived with her family in a cottage in Stoney Middleton. She was courting a young man named William Barnsley who also lived in the small village, and as the courtship continued, it was expected that a wedding would be imminent. However, as Hannah was contemplating being a bride, William's feelings changed and he called off the affair.

Hannah was devastated and unable to contemplate life without William, she decided to end it all. She climbed up the steep limestone rocks of Middleton Dale where supposedly and rather theatrically she declared –

'Oh my William! My William – false William – no I will not call thee false! My love! My life! Never, never again will mine eyes behold thee – thee whom I loved – ah! I love thee still! Oh my love, wilt thou not come to my grave, and shed one tear to the memory of her, who died for thee? I'll bless thee again my love and then from this dizzy height I'll cast myself and prove to thee and the world – my love is stronger than death. I sink, I go, my love, my love.'

By this time she had undoubtedly attracted quite a crowd as standing on the edge, she leapt into thin air. But the theatrical display was not over. Miraculously, the voluminous skirts and petticoats she was wearing billowed out as she launched herself off the cliff face, acting like a parachute. This undoubtedly slowed her descent and saved her life but as she fell she struck against rocks, landed in a thorny bush and lost consciousness. Horrified onlookers rushed to help and carried her bloody body to her home where slowly she recovered.

Unfortunately, she only lived for a few more years. She died on December 12th 1764 and was buried in the local churchyard on December 12th 1764. Although her tomb is now illegible, the Stoney Middleton parish register contains the record of her baptism on February 22nd 1738 and of her burial. She had remained a spinster and left a small fortune of £180.

Continue up the hill for approximately 100m until you see a stile on your left leading to a path up a grassy hill. Cross the stile and continue up this path. Just over the brow of the hill and beyond the trees on the right, note the boundary stone on your right – 8.

How many people must have made a wish at this particularly poignant stone. It is a sandstone boulder pierced with a pattern of holes in which money was placed in payment for medicines and other supplies needed by the quarantined victims of Eyam during the period of the plague. Like so many such plague landmarks in other towns and parishes, it is sometimes called the Vinegar stone or penny stone because vinegar was poured into the holes in the belief that this would sterilise the coins.

Continue to a stone wall opposite and go through the stile into a field at the end of which is a stile, then an enclosed path. after passing through a further stile, continue across two fields and head straight on along the walled track until meeting a surfaced road and houses. You will shortly see the Lydgate Graves – 9 – on your left. When you reach The Square in the heart of Eyam turn left and return to the car park along Church Street which is the start/end of this walk.

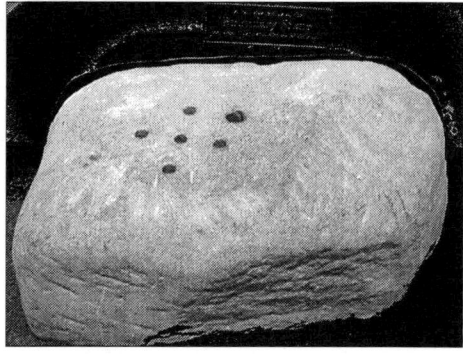

The boundary stone pierced with a pattern of holes in which money was placed

7: Riley Graves – Stoke – Froggatt Bridge – Stoney Middleton – Lydgate Graves

THE GHOST AT THE GRAVES – PHANTOM FIGURE OF FLORA – SPECTRE CROSSING – HAUNTED HALL – HIGHWAYMAN'S HAUNTS – STRANGE SMELLS AT THE HALL – RED RETURNS

5¼ miles (8·50km)

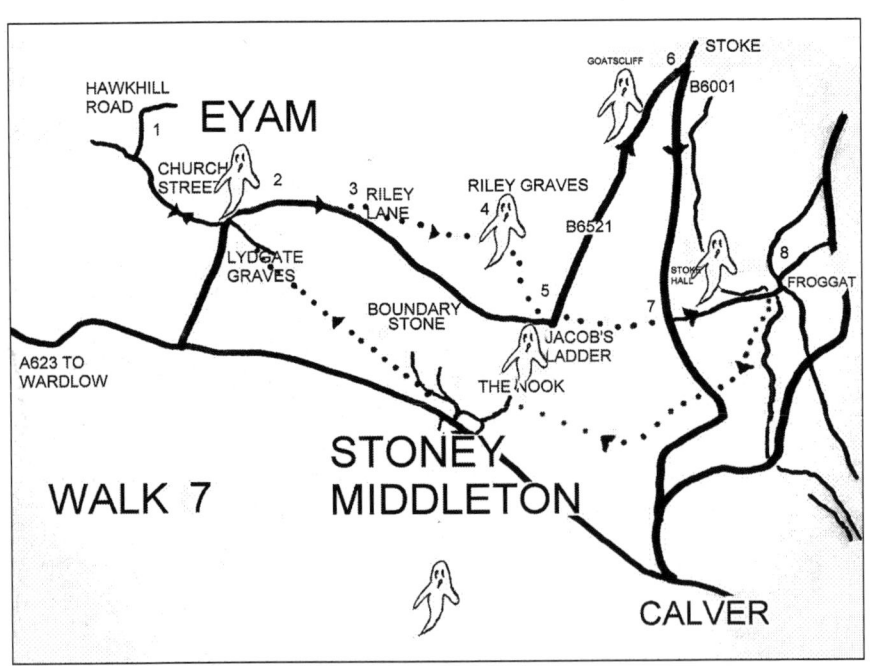

The Walk

To begin our walk, follow points 1-5 and the directions given in *Walk 6* from Eyam, past the Riley Graves and onto the Eyam to Grindleford Road B6521. Now watch out!

> In the 1970's the father of a young Grindleford businessman told Clarence Daniel of his son's experience when driving along this road from Eyam to Grindleford. He returned home shaken and upset. On the journey he had seen an indistinct figure shrouded in cloak and hood, cross the road from the top of Jacob's Ladder, an old bridle-road climbing steeply from Stoney Middleton. He had stopped his car and watched the figure pass through the solid stone wall to proceed up the old cart-track in the direction of the disused Riley slate-pits. Shocked and dazed by the experience, he sat at the wheel for some time questioning whether the combination of isolation, tiredness and monotonous visual stimuli had generated an Hallucination – a word that comes from a Greek term meaning 'to wander in the mind', yet he dismissed this. What he had seen was no formless wraiths or insubstantial spirit image wreathed in a shroud-like astral attire. It had the appearance of physical solidity, clothed in garments which had a realistic quality; the type of attire that would have been worn by the phantom during the days of their mortality.

In *Walk 5* we told you the story of Flora, the ghostly young woman who is said to wander round here, and our next stop is the classical statue of Flora, the Greek goddess of flowers, hidden away in a small plantation at Goatscliff.

To visit the statue, leave point 5, turn left and continue down this road for ¾ mile (1·20km) until just before reaching the B6001 – 6. Climb over the wall stile just before the farm drive on your left. Walk up through the trees for about 100 yards. It used to be difficult to find but on a recent visit, the shrubbery and surrounding trees had been cleared, so just head up the hill parallel to the drive to Goatscliff Farm.

The statue of Fair Flora

There are various stories woven around this statue and why she should be sited in such a remote place, but I prefer the sad ballad entitled *The Astrologer's Daughter* by J Castle Hall which links the statue with this story:-

A gypsy girl named Flora fell in love with Victor, the son of the local squire. They married and set up home together in a small cottage near Grindleford close to the woods where they had met, and for a time they were extremely happy, then Victor had to go away to war. Twelve months passed before Victor returned to find the cottage abandoned. He was mystified yet as he looked around, he saw his wife coming towards him. She was dressed in the purest white garments; her arms were outstretched but as he ran to embrace her, his arms passed through her outline as if it was a shadow. He had seen her ghost.

He later found that Flora had died giving birth to a baby daughter adopted by the gypsies, so in her memory Victor erected the statue of Flora on the site where they met. Her ghost is still said to haunt the area, and some say that when the moon is full, her statue comes alive.

After viewing the statue, return to the junction of the B6001, turn right and walk past Stoke Hall until reaching a lane on your left – 7.

If you do not wish to view the statue, leave point 5, turn left towards the bend, and cross the B6521 road to the gate opposite. The views from here are quite stunning.

Go through the gate and the land starts to fall as you head down the fields towards the road in the bottom which is difficult to see at this point. Keep the wall on your

The impressive view of Froggatt, Curbar and Baslow Edge

left, and when you reach the next gate go over a stile at the side and straight down the field to a stile onto the B6001 – 7 which runs from Calver to Grindleford.

Former occupants of a farm on the outskirts of Grindleford often found their son chuckling at the antics of a little man in his bedroom. As only he

> could see the little man they put it down to his active imagination, not realising that children and animals are particularly sensitive to paranormal activity. One evening they saw the electric light hanging from the centre of the room swinging and the boy started to laugh. The parents could see no possible reason for the light to swing or the boy to laugh until he told them that the little man had just hit the lamp with his stick. On another occasion, although there was no breeze, the curtain kept billowing out, and according to the boy, the little man was pulling them about.

Before resuming our walk look to your left across the road and amongst the trees is Stoke Hall, an impressive 18th century house standing on the wooded banks of the River Derwent. It is a handsome stone-built Georgian residence with substantial additions and outbuildings, built in 1755 as the Peakland home of the Earl of Bradford. It was let to Robert Arkwright, son of Sir Richard Arkwright, then later turned into a hotel, restaurant and night-club before reverting back to private housing.

Stoke Hall is extremely haunted

Cross the B6001 and walk down the lane opposite where over on your left you can look over the lawn of Stoke Hall where the classical statue of Flora that we've just encountered could have stood. There are numerous stories weaved around this statue linking it with Stoke Hall. Some say that it was erected in memory of a tragic accident that befell the daughter of the house, or in another version it's a Victorian maid called Flora who was murdered at the hall. The statue could have been a gift from the Duke of Devonshire to a member of the Bridgeman family or to a Mrs Taylor who had admired the statue while visiting Chatsworth. But the arrival of the statue at Stoke Hall coincided with a spell of bad luck, then one moonlit evening as Mrs Taylor looked over the shadowy lawn, she was alarmed to see the motionless statue, silvered by moonlight had taken on a ghostly quality and appeared to be moving. This so freaked Mrs Taylor that the statue was hastily removed from the grounds of the hall, but rather than returning it to Chatsworth, for some reason it was hauled half a mile away, across the road and up a steep hillside to be placed in total isolation surrounded by trees.

There are so many stories of hauntings at Stoke Hall that it is now virtually impossible to substantiate them. According to an old source, the neighbouring folk feared to pass after dark and one of the reasons was the story of a skull that haunted the upper storey.

In a rather gloomy passage in what were the old servants quarters, rustling noises and strange whispers were frequently heard and in such an atmosphere of fear and unease it was hard to retain domestic staff.

In former years a member of staff of Stoke Hall used to tell of an heiress to the property being murdered in the Hall, (that would tie in with one of the statue stories) and spoke of indelible blood stains and a haunted room in which neither the family, guests or servants were asked to sleep. In the 1880's a guest saw a ghostly lady in a beautiful flowing dress coming down the stairs, but the lady had no head and disappeared as the watcher screamed and fainted.

A guest saw a headless lady coming down the stairs

It is not infrequent for the servant's bells to ring mysteriously and the burglar-alarm triggers without any explanation. In the 1970's the hall was converted into a hotel and the owners at the time experienced strange and inexplicable phenomena which suggested that some ghostly entities still haunt the hall. On one occasion, a workman had agreed to meet the owners to discuss what work needed to be done. While he waited in the kitchen, the bells began to ring, yet he was alone in the house. On another occasion, the burglar alarm which is triggered by a movement censor suddenly rang, but despite a full search, nothing was found.

As you wander down the lane, look out for odd shaped trees

Old Ned was a carrier who lived in the vicinity of Stoke Hall, but poor Ned suffered from severe depression and decided to end it all by hanging himself. He made many attempts on the surrounding trees, but one after another, the boughs gave way. Finally he succeeded in ending his life in

> an old barn a few hundred yards from Stoke Hall by the side of the River Derwent. Now in ruin, people say that around midnight the ghost of Old Ned can still be seen with a rope, tearing off the branches of the trees before finally disappearing into the ruins of the old barn. There's also the story that all those trees where the boughs broke are now deformed.

Continue until reaching the delightful little Froggat Bridge and the hamlet of Froggatt – 8. Just before the bridge go through the small gate or climb over the wall stile on your right, and follow the footpath through the woods.

The lane leading to Froggat Bridge

Froggatt Bridge

The footpath through the woods

Follow this delightful path with the River Derwent on your left. Go through the first stile and walk diagonally across a field up to the top right hand corner. Cross the stile in the corner of the field just up from the gate, then turn immediately right and head up the field keeping a wall on your right towards a farm building. At the top of the field go through a small gate which brings you back onto the B6001 – 9.

> During the late 17th century, the inns and ale-houses of the Peak District were frequented by the notorious highwayman John Nevison of

Pontefact. One market day he was in the Castle Hotel in Bakewell where he got chatting to a poor tenant farmer from Padley just north of Grindleford. The farmer had just sold some cattle to pay his quarterly rent at Michaelmas, and was celebrating his shrewd bargaining with a few strong pints of autumn ale. He was quite happy to accept more from a friendly stranger who asked him the way to Sheffield, and all caution gone, the tipsy farmer told the stranger that the quickest route was past his house, He then proposed that they should travel together as they'd be company for each other and offer added protection against highwaymen. The well-dressed stranger agreed and they set off from Bakewell as the sun was sinking low.

Taking the Hassop road, they travelled in silence until they reached Calver Sough where they allowed their horses to rest for a few minutes before the next stage of the journey to Tomlin's Gate. The farmer admired the strangers fine horse to which he replied 'Aye. It's best to be well mounted when the roads are lonely and robbers are abroad.'

As they rode towards Stoke Hall, under the dark beech trees, the stranger produced a pistol and pressed it to the farmers chest, ordering him to hand over his money.

'Please don't take my money,' sobbed the befuddled farmer. 'I sold my cows to pay the rent at Michaelmas. It's all the money I have in the world, and if you take it I'll be thrown off my farm. I have a wife and family and we'll be paupers if I can't pay.'

John Nevison said nothing, but pressed harder with the pistol, clicking back the hammer as he did so. With a heavy heart, the farmer reached inside his coat and brought out the canvas bag containing the gold.

'If this is indeed the rent money as you say, you shall have it back, you have my word upon that, but I have need of it now and you have ten days till Michaelmas.' As he spoke, Nevison snatched the bag from the farmer and rode off.

The farmer had ten days to lament his lost gold, but as he sat late on the tenth night thinking he'd soon have neither hearth nor home, he heard a horse galloping up from Grindleford bridge. Reaching his house, it reigned in briefly and there was a smash as something flew through the window. Lying on the floor amongst the broken glass was a canvas bag and inside was the money Nevison had taken from the farmer, plus an extra guinea wrapped in a scrap of paper. On the paper was written 'Interest for the loan of rent money'.

John Nevison, Gentleman of the Road had kept his word, but does he also return to the scene. Many people have reported seeing a ghostly rider galloping along this road, and his description fits that of a highwayman.

Cross the B6001 and go up the lane to Knouchy Farm. As you reach the farm buildings on your left, the footpath bears right and passes alongside these buildings. Ignore the gateway on your right but go through the gateway ahead and when you reach the edge of the farm buildings turn left, ignoring the path going straight on. Walk down the side of the building to reach a field. Facing south towards Calver village, bear right towards a pair of gates in the middle of a wall. Cross over a stile by the gate and with the wall on your right walk along the path as it descends a slope then opens out into a field. Keep on the main path heading in the direction of Stoney Middleton until at the end of the path, go through a small gate and turn left onto a surfaced road – 10. On your right are the Roman Baths. Follow the road round the church and into The Bank.

Ignoring the road on your left which leads to the A623, follow the minor road as it bears right then at the junction of The Fold and Cliff Bottom – 11, take the latter and walk up the hill. Continue for approximately 100m until you see a stile on your left leading to a path up a grassy hill. Cross the stile and continue up this path,

This charming old phoyograph taken in The Nook at the turn of the 19/20th century

passing the boundary stone and continuing along the path back to Eyam.

Turn left and return to the car park along Church Street which is the start/end of this walk.

8: Lydgate – Stoney Middleton – Sallet Hole Mine – Black Harry Gate – Eyam Dale

Ghostly Mines – Haunt of the Highwaymen – Ghostly Old Woman & a Phantom Cyclist

5 miles (8·10km)

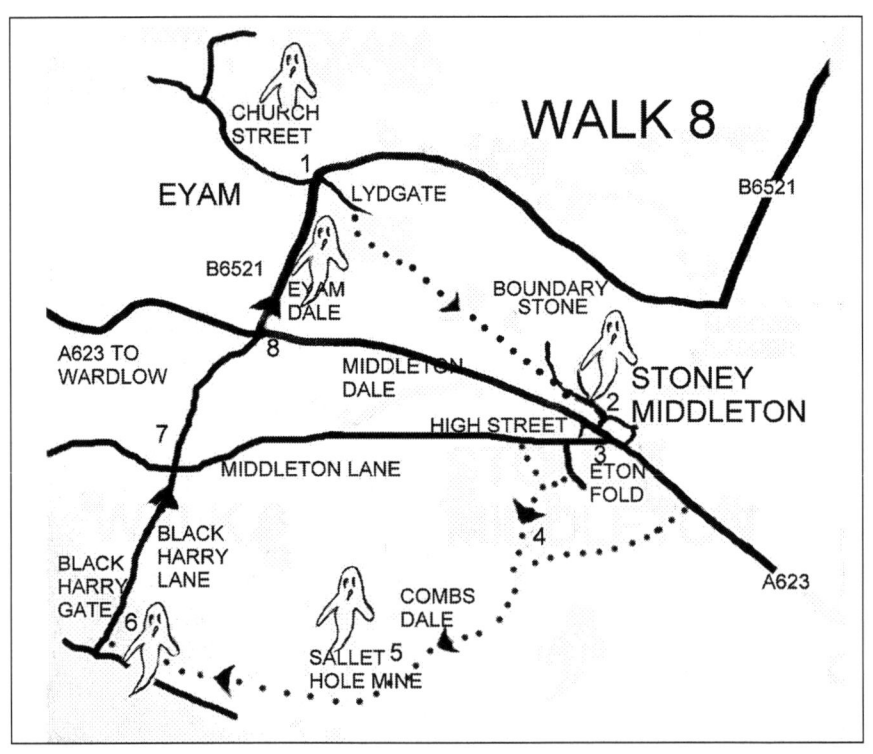

The Walk

This walk begins at The Square at the Town End of Eyam – 1. From here, take the narrow lane called Lydgate by the side of the telephone box and post box. This was the old main road from Eyam into the village of Stoney Middleton before the road was cut through Eyam Dale in the 19th century. Lyd or Lid is a Saxon word which means to cover or protect, and at its entrance was a strong gate at which 'watch and ward' was kept every night between 9 p.m and 6 a.m. Every able bodied, male householder in the village was officially bound to take a turn at this gate to question anyone entering the village. As watchman he had a large wooden halbert or watch-bill for protection, and when he came off duty in the morning, he took the watch-bill and reared it against the door of the next watcher. This custom was practiced into the 18th century with Eyam being one of the last villages to retain this very ancient ritual.

As you walk along Lydgate, on your right is Rose and Fossil Cottage. During the time of the plague, this was the home of John and Francis Wood and ironically, two hundred years later it became the home of William Wood, Eyam historian and village chronicler, unrelated to the previous occupants.

A few yards further, we reach Lydgate Cottage.

By the side of Lydgate Cottage are the 1666 plague graves of Thomas and Mary Darby in a small, walled enclosure which was once part of the Parson's field – a piece of Glebe land now occupied by a small housing estate. These are known as The Lydgate Graves. George Darby died on July 4th 1666 and his daughter Mary aged 20 died on September 4th. Tradition says that Mary Darby was seized by the plague as she gathered flowers for her fathers grave and died the following day, but George's wife survived and died in 1674.

A hundred yards further, on the right is The Rock, the former home of Clarence Daniel, the Eyam antiquarian and lifelong resident of Eyam whose ancestors survived the plague. From early youth he avidly collected everything associated with his native village and in 1976 achieved his dearest ambition of opening a small, private museum at The Rock, to display the treasures which he had accumulated throughout his life. After his death in 1987, his wife Cecily donated his collection to the Eyam Village Society, in the hope, now realised that it would inspire the foundation of a museum. The Eyam Museum opened in 1994 and is opposite the Hawkhill car park

Head straight on along the walled track, signed – Stoney Middleton & Boundary Stone. Follow the track through two fields. Pass through a squeeze stile onto an enclosed path at the end of which is another squeeze stile. Follow the signs across the next field which was formerly common land where isolated huts were built for the accommodation of the plague victims. Follow the footpath directly across this field where you will see the boundary stone on your left near a ring of trees.

During the plague, this would have been the route taken by carters and the setting for another plague related story concerning a carrier from Bubnell. The Duke of Devonshire had instructed a Bubnell carter who worked on the Chatsworth estate to convey a load of timber to Eyam – or somewhere in the vicinity. Upon the appointed day, the carter arrived at his destination but was unable to obtain assistance in unloading the wagon, so in the steady drizzle of rain, he unloaded it single handed and returned to Bubnell soaked to the skin and chilled to the bone. When the unfortunate man started to cough and sneeze, the initial symptoms of the plague, his terrified neighbours barricaded him in his house. One neighbour even threatened to shoot him if he so much as tried to cross his threshold and rumours that the carter had brought the plague to Bubnell flew round the area. Eventually this was brought to the attention of the Earl of Devonshire who arranged that his personal physician should examine the man to diagnose his complaint. Taking no risks, the patient was instructed to stand on the Bubnell side of the river Derwent while the doctor questioned him from the other side. Never was such a strange examination conducted, but eventually the doctor was confident that the carter had nothing more than a cold and he was allowed out of quarantine.

Follow the path bearing slightly right down the steep hillside to reach the lane on the outskirts of Stoney Middleton, then follow it through the village before turning right to the T junction with the A623 which at this point is known as The Avenue – 2.

Friendly rivalry has existed between the folks of Eyam and Stoney Middleton for centuries. Eyam youths would rouse the indignation of those from Stoney Middleton by calling – *Middleton scrubs, wash their faces in Eyam dolly-tubs*. Not sure what the response was!

Then there's the old rural rhyme –

Baslow for gentlefolks, Calver for trenchers
Middleton for rogues and thieves, and Eyam for pretty wenches

This slur on the folks of Stoney Middleton goes back a few centuries when the village had more than its fair share of seedy boarding houses frequented by tramps and navvies, but for those who couldn't afford a night's accommodation there was always a warm alternative. Homeless men and women spent the winter nights sleeping on the edge of the lime kilns that burnt in the Dale, enjoying the treacherous luxury of the warmth generated by the burning lime. Sadly many were accidentally cremated because if the wind changed direction, the sleepers could either be suffocated or overcome by the fumes, and many rolled into the furnace below.

A drawing of the smelting house in Middleton Dale by Frances Chantrey 1817

By 1808 crime had become such a problem that the Eyam and Stoney Middleton Society for the Prosecution of Felons was set up to keep law and order, a job which was handed over to the modern police force in 1857.

The village street, Stoney Middleton, early 19th century by Frances Chantrey

Around the mid 18th century there was a large number of itinerant tinkers, hawkers, pedlars and general ne'er-do-wells who toured the country visiting fairs and wakes weeks selling cheap trinkets. One such pedlar was a Scots man who arrived for the Eyam Wakes around 1750, and although he had a licence to operate he was disliked by the local pedlars who tried to undercut him. This no doubt annoyed the Scottish pedlar who decided to report the others for trading without licenses, because even then it was illegal for street traders to operate without a licence. As the other pedlars were ordered out of the parish, they vowed to get revenge on their informant, a conversation that was overheard by the landlord of The Bull's Head who at the end of Wakes week, sent someone to accompany the Scottish pedlar as far as Stoney Middleton. But instead of leaving the area, the pedlar stopped off at the Moon Inn, further up the main road and the opposite side of the road to the present Moon Inn. Apparently the inn gets its name from an old village tale about a simple villagers who attempted to take the moon's reflection out of the mill-dam, under the impression that it was a cheese.

It was there at the Moon Inn that the rival pedlars murdered the Scottish pedlar. They then took his body by horseback to Cael's Wark (Carlswark Cave), near Lovers Leap in Middleton Dale where it was discovered about 20 years later by a man called Peter Morton who was led there after a dream. The body was only recognisable because of his attire, and the bones and buckle shoes were boxed up and kept in Eyam church. After a number of years when no-one had claimed them, the nameless peddler was buried in the churchyard and a bell-ringer named Matthew Hall took the shoes. No one was ever charged for the murder.

When the lead mines began to decline and the fires were extinguished on the lead kilns, Stoney Middleton went into slow decline. First the millers and maltsters, then the blacksmith's forge, the manufacturers of farm boots, besoms and barrels. Just over a century ago, Thomas Furness and Thomas Goddard carried on a business as tallow-chandlers. Sixty years ago, people could still remember the frame from which the wicks

The Moon Inn

were suspended as the chandler alternatively raised and lowered them into a vat of molten tallow. Each dip added another coat of tallow to increase the candle's thickness and its price which was determined by the number of times it had been dipped.

According to the 1851 census, the village had 134 houses with a population of 593 although this was rather misleading as all the houses north of the stream that divides the village were included in Eyam parish. In 1851 there were nine public houses, but during the next century six of them ceased to hold licences.

To continue our walk, cross the A623 to the Moon Inn on the corner of High Street. A plain and unpretentious cross stands at the foot of the hill, although once an oil lamp occupied the iron frame with which it is surmounted. It was erected to commemorate the repeal of the Corn Laws in 1846. As you climb up High Street its easy to see why in 1664-5, when Robert Ashton was High Sheriff of the county he had no coach and when asked why, he replied 'because the town where I live stands on one end.'

Follow High Street until reaching Eton Fold on your left. This becomes a track as you follow it out of the village. Follow the signs through a gate by the side of a driveway and the grassy track through two fields, then just before some barns where the track forks, head left over a stile signed to Coombs Dale, then right to the stile in the fence about 25 yards to the left of the barns. Follow the direction of arrows across the field, on a path that bears to the right, then eventually drops down towards Coombs Dale, an attractive steep sided dale dotted with old mine workings – 4. Lead was certainly mined in Derbyshire before the arrival of the Romans in 45 AD., and stimulated by the demand during the 16th and 17th centuries, lead mining expanded to become a major industry in the limestone country of Derbyshire of which Eyam is right in the centre.

> Many mines are haunted by strange, eerie noises that escape from the rocks. There is a close correlation between them and the lights, humming noises and other paranormal phenomena reported in this area. All mines were thought to be inhabited by spirits, often referred to as the little people who were held responsible for any casualties or unexplained incidents occurring in or around the mines. They are also purportedly haunted by eerie, mystical presences of long dead miners. Tales of mysterious sightings, noises and unexplained phenomena were passed verbally so it is not surprising to find that ghost stories and tales of strange sightings were rife amongst the mining communities and have been handed down through generations of miners.

Turn left over a stile and at the bottom of the steep sided Coombs Dale you'll reach a plank foot-bridge across a rushing stream muddied by quarry workings. Here you will join a lane which runs through the dale for 1½ miles until reaching Coombs Lane – 5.

Coombs Dale

Follow this round and after about ¾ mile you pass Sallet Hole Mine on your right. The Sallet Hole Mine was operational until a few years ago producing quality fluorspar used in the steel industry. The fenced off flooded mine level cuts deep into the hillside, although nature is reclaiming the landscape.

> While working at Sallet Hole Mine, Mr Bernard Marshall believes that he saw the spectre of the mine. At the time, Bernard was working in the 'Unwin Vein' with a foreman electrician who was reluctant to confirm or deny the happening although he was prepared to admit there was definitely someone or something there. Bernard was however adamant that the figure he saw was wearing a long check coat and a flat cap, hardly the usual attire of his contemporaries, and mine regulations insist upon all underground workers wearing of a safety helmet not a cap. As he watched it simply vanished from sight.
>
> Other miners have encountered these spectres who seem to be condemned to wander for ever in the underground galleries and Sallet Hole Mine is said to be haunted by an old man wearing a cap and long coat, He is accompanied by a dog. They both disappear when approached. Black dogs are said to dwell in mines and caves and are often seen only as fire-coloured eyes with a dark, ominous shape behind them.

Leave Sallet Hole Mine and follow the lane through Coombs Dale. After about ¾ mile you will reach Black Harry Gate – 6, named after a highwayman called Black Harry who in the early 18th century, frequently attacked and robbed the packhorse trains that crossed the moors in this area between Tideswell and Bakewell.

The archetypal highway man was born in the aftermath of the Civil War when the execution of Charles I in 1649 left many Royalist officers without any means of support. Because they were unaccustomed to earning a living and had no trade to fall back on, they took to the high road.

That's why the highwayman is often portrayed as a romantic figure attired in fancy clothes; an aristocrat amongst thieves who just happened to be down on his luck. It's therefore not surprising that the highwayman became a popular folk hero, especially amongst the poor who had nothing to fear from such a person as they seldom travelled and more importantly had nothing worth stealing.

Although most were ruthless cut-throats, some seem to have been personified as dashing young gentlemen who rode round the country stealing nothing from a pretty maid but a kiss, but that's the romantic image, and the mystique that surrounds the highwayman owes much to this supposed chivalry and gallantry to ladies, his illicit affairs and his numerous narrow escapes.

The highwayman Black Harry was so notorious his name was given to the area where his ghost is still seen

The unarmed post-boys who carried the mail on horseback, frequently at night to avoid being held up by slow moving herds of animals, were a prime target for the highwaymen, and robberies were frequent. The post-boys were often suspected of being in league with the highway men and the Post Office advised anyone sending bank drafts or valuable documents to cut them in half and send each piece separately.

> In 1722, the death penalty was imposed for being armed and disguised on high roads and open heaths. Black Harry was eventually arrested by the Castleton Bow Street Runners and was hung drawn and quartered at the Gallows Tree at Wardlow Mires.. Gibbeting the corpse was popular right up until the mid 19th century and regularly took place at Wardlow one of three gibbet sites in the area
>
> It's said that the ghost of the intrepid Black Harry still haunts the area. On a dark, windy night it's easy to image he's still there; the black-clad figure complete with tricorn hat and cloak slung over his shoulder, but witnesses always describe him as having no face.

Leave Black Harry Gate and turn right into Black Harry Lane. After about 1 mile you will reach cross-roads at Lane Head – 7. Middleton Lane goes off to the right and Moisty Lane to the left, but go straight across and continue for about half a mile, passing the entrance to Darlton Quarry on your left until arriving at the main A623 road – 8.

Cross the A623 and take the B6521 road opposite going north/east. This is Eyam Dale.

During the plague, this would have been a dropping off place for carters organised by the Duke of Devonshire. Brick ovens were built at Bubnell where bread was said to have been baked then brought to the bottom of Eyam Dale, paid for by money sterilised in the brook. The site of the kneading trough and bakehouse are marked on old maps.

According to an account by White Watson, 'the brook near Stockingcote was called Monday Brook because during the plague year, the people of Eyam who would normally have gone to Bakewell's Monday market, seven miles away could go no further. They dropped their money into this riverlet in exchange for goods.

In 1814, some labourers employed in burning limestone in Eyam Dale, found a great quantity of silver and copper coins bearing the inscriptions of Roman emperors like Probus, Gallienus and Victorinus. The Romans were certainly interested in the lead that was mined in this area, and Roman remains have been found in abundance in the neighbourhood of Eyam and Stoney Middleton. In the dale, there have been Roman coins, shards of pottery and a pair of silver armilla – now in Weston Park Museum.

> Eyam Dale really does have its share of ghostly tales. Do you remember the story of the ghostly old woman who was responsible for stripping the bed clothes off sleeping occupants in a cottage in Eyam Dale? There's the additional story of a tipsy lead-miner named Tom Loxley who had an encounter with the spectre after earlier expressing his disbelief and lack of fear of such apparitions. He had been drinking in the Golden Ball Inn that used to stand at the Stoney Middleton side of Eyam Dale and his journey was along the route you are just about to take. (See *Walk 1*)
>
> If you're not concerned about meeting the phantom figure described as 'rather more than middle aged, wearing a short bed gown, linsey petticoat, mobbed cap and shoes with shiny buckles', watch out for the phantom cyclist.

Two men were walking up Eyam Dale one morning after an early morning rabbit-shoot when they had to leap hurriedly aside to avoid being run over by a cyclist racing down the steep gradient. Turning to curse the cyclist, the men were shocked to see that the road was completely deserted.

Down this same stretch of road one dark night, a man was walking home when he distinctly heard the swish of the rubber tyres and ringing of a bicycle bell. He turned to stare in the direction of the noise but could see nothing.

This old photograph from the beginning of the last century shows Castle Rock, said to be the site of a Roman fort. One of the buildings on the site is the Golden Ball Inn where Tom Loxley had been drinking. The scene is totally unrecognisable today

'What idiot is riding down here without lights?' he muttered to himself as he stepped aside but the cyclist never materialised.

A man and his wife were walking along Stoney Middleton Dale when they heard a cyclist approaching from behind. They instinctively stepped into the side to let it pass just as a Chesterfield service bus approached from the opposite direction. The bus rounded a bend and swept the road with its headlights but there was no sign of a cyclist.

The phantom cyclist was actually seen by a keen cyclist as he laboriously climbed the ascent of Eyam Dale one very wet day. Dripping with water and making hard work of the climb, the cyclist was amazed to see another cyclist effortlessly overtake him and pull away. Not only that, the phantom cyclist was bone dry despite the fact that it was pouring with rain.

At the head of Eyam Dale you will arrive in The Square which is the start/end of this walk.

9: Calver – Froggatt – Curbar

PROTECTIVE DOGS – THE PRETEND CORPSE – PHANTOM FOOTSTEPS – MINE SPIRITS & THE PUMPING ENGINE

7¾ miles (12·55km) or from Calver 3¾ miles (6·05km)

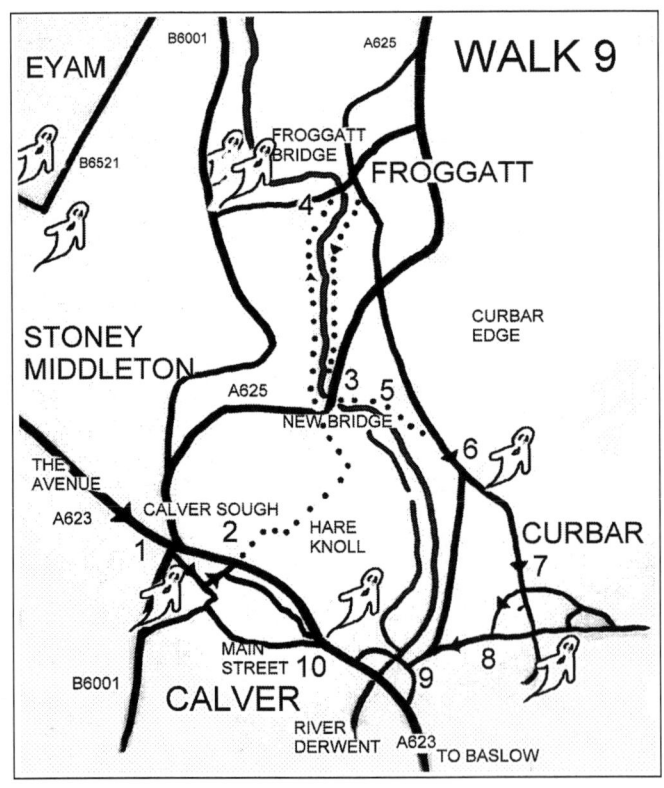

The Walk

This walk can begin at either Eyam or Calver. If you prefer to walk from Eyam, (7¾ miles – 12·55km) go to The Square, walk along Lydgate, past the Lydgate graves and the boundary stone and down into Stoney Middleton as in *Walk 8*. Turn right to join the main A623 road and turn left to walk along this stretch which is called the Avenue.

> A Methodist Minister was walking along this road from Calver to Stoney Middleton one night when he realised he was being followed. He was carrying the collection money from the various chapels he served and he felt rather vulnerable until he was unexpectedly joined by a large dog that stayed protectively by his heels until he reached his destination. Reaching down to pat the dog, his hand passed straight through it.

At Calver Sough cross-roads – 1 – turn right into the B6001, then immediately left into Sough Lane. If you are starting your walk from Calver, park down near the cricket ground where the road is wider. (This walk will be 3¾ miles – 6·05km.) Look ahead, slightly to your right and perched on the hill is the Derwent Water Arms.

> Many years ago, a landlord of the Derwent Arms was in the habit of playing practical jokes. One evening he lay on the parlour table and got his wife to cover him with a sheet. She was then instructed to go into the bar and tell his customers he had died suddenly.
>
> Naturally the customers expressed their condolences and the wife invited them into the parlour to pay their respects to the 'corpse'. They gathered round the table in a sympathetic silence then suddenly the 'deceased' sat up and terrified his audience.
>
> However, the following day the landlord was driving to Bakewell in his horse-drawn trap when the horse suddenly shied. The man was thrown and broke his neck, so that evening, he actually lay on the same table, but this time he was a genuine corpse.

Derwentwater Arms, haunted by a previous landlord

> Various landlords have since reported hearing unexplained footsteps and being aware of an inexplicable presence. Regular visitors would not stay in one of the bedrooms and deciding to investigate, the landlady and her niece slept in there one night. They occupied the double bed and a maid had a single bed in the corner. At midnight, the door opened and a menacing presence entered the room. It stopped to view the occupants walked round the bed, paused again then left the room. Could it be the ghost of that landlord playing another of his practical jokes?

With the cricket ground on your left, walk to the end of it, then turn left into Donkey Lane until reaching the T junction with the main A623 – 2. Turn right and cross the road shortly afterwards to follow the opposite track uphill. Stay on this as it bears right. After 200 yards turn sharp left and 125 yards later, cross the step-over stile on your right. This is Hare Knoll and by now you should have great views of Curbar Edge, the outcrop of gritstone rocks on the horizon a mile or so away.

Walk beside the wall on your left through the first field to reach a ruined building in the second field. Cross the stile and walk down the right side of the third field into the bottom corner. Whilst still in the field, turn left passing a gate-way on your right 100 yard later. Aim for the stile on the left side of the wall on the opposite side of the field. Descend the path beyond to the road, the A625 at New Bridge – 3.

Cross the road and walk beside the River Derwent on your right for 750m, crossing Stoke Brook by a footbridge and bear right. Continue along this delightful riverside path for about half a mile until reaching Froggatt Bridge – 4.

*Froggatt Bridge
with its two dissimilar arches*

Cross the bridge and head towards the hamlet of Froggatt

Froggatt Bridge is unusual in having two dissimilar arches. On the village side is a larger, pointed arch dating from the 17th century, and next to it is a smaller rounded arch which was probably added to extend the bridge when the river was widened to enable it to be dammed for the use of Calver Mill.

Cross the bridge and go right into Riddings Lane, then join the riverside path along the eastern bank of the River Derwent. Continue until reaching New Bridge and the A625.

Cross the road and continue bearing left beyond the weir, up the bank and over the next field – 5. Turn right at the road that leads into Curbar keeping left at the junction into The Bent – 6 until reaching Pinfold Hill on your right – 7.

A young woman from Eyam had, just before the plague, married a resident of Curbar where she had taken up residency, but her widowed mother was still in Eyam. The young woman secretly visited the stricken village and on the last occasion found her mother dying of the plague. She returned hastily to Curbar, but within two days had herself developed the fatal symptoms and died in agony. To the great relief of her neighbours many of whom remembered how the plague had raged in Curbar thirty years previously, the disease did not spread.

When she was twelve years old, Gail Sharpe stayed with her grandmother in an old cottage in Curbar. It was early on the morning of June 10th 1970 when Gail suddenly woke to hear someone in her room talking. She pulled herself up and saw an old woman sitting on the end of her bed. The woman wore steel-rimmed spectacles and her grey hair was parted down the middle and pulled back into a bun at the back. Round her shoulders was a black knitted shawl over a black dress. According to Gail she also wore a smile and looked very pleasant, but Gail buried her head under the bedclothes until she felt calm enough to peep out. Much to her relief the old woman had gone and Gail fled downstairs in a distressed state.

Both Gail and her grandmother were convinced that there was something eerie about the cottage. Footsteps were often heard crossing the landing and passing through the bedroom. Gail claimed that there was a whirlwind in the warmest room of the cottage and a feeling of chill in most of its rooms. When Mr George Goddard, a former Parish Council chairman and churchwarden was informed of these events and heard the description of the old lady, he immediately identified the woman as a former occupant of the cottage.

Walk down Pinfold Hill and at the T junction with Hill Road turn right downhill towards Calver – 8. Ahead of you you'll see Calver mill which was originally built as a corn mill operated by the water of the River Derwent. In 1785 it became a cotton mill but was burnt down in 1802. A new mill was built 1803/4, but this ceased work as a mill in the 1920's.

Calver Mill was originally operated by the water power of the River Derwent

After acting as a storage depot in the second world war, it was taken over by Sissons of Sheffield who made stainless steel sinks. It is now converted into private apartments, but if any building should be haunted this is it! With seven storeys, a large central pediment at the front and staircase turrets at the back, the sinister proportions of this 'dark satanic mill' were ideal as the outside of Colditz in the 1970's BBC serial of that name. Not all the locals were happy with this, as while filming was taking places, it was necessary to fly the swastika over the valley.

At the road junction with the Bridge Inn across the road – 9 – turn left to meet the A623 Baslow Road. This area is known as Calver Bridge and forms the boundary between Calver and Curbar.

> A young woman was travelling on foot between Calver and Calver Bridge late one night. There was no street lighting or pavements and the hedges and overhanging trees formed strange shapes and made even stranger noises as she hurried past. Her imagination was playing tricks and she was quaking with fear as she almost ran headlong into a large, white dog that seemed to appear from nowhere. Although usually afraid of dogs, she found this one to be friendly and comforting and it stayed with her until the lights of houses were reached when, with a wag of its tail, it went its own way, disconcertingly disappearing through a solid stone wall.

Cross the road with care and follow Main Street – 10 – through the village. Note the cottages that would have housed the lead miners, working in the mines which this area was so reliant upon.

The Main Street, Calver

All lead mines were believed to be inhabited by mine spirits thought to be the ghosts of miners who have died underground – see also *Walk 3 & 8*. Benign in nature, some mine spirits were mischievous and enjoyed frustrating the miners, but they were generally helpful as long as they were treated with respect. Gifts of food and drink were frequently left for them, and I came across a lady who remembered her mother preparing pastry filled pasties which her father took down the mine for his 'snap'. In the pastry she always cut his initials on the left corner, the portion he would leave in the mine to placate the spirits of the mine.

They were often referred to as the Knockers because their hammers could be heard tapping deep in the workings. They would tap to indicate when a miner was approaching a rich seam, or tap three times to warn of death, or guide rescuers to the location of cave-ins. If insulted they could cause rock showers of cave-ins and these supernatural creatures were held responsible for any casualties or unexplained incidents occurring in or around the mines. For this reason, when a pumping engine at Calver didn't work properly, the miners laid rowan branches on it, hoping to counteract the mischief of the little people who they believed had stopped it functioning.

Continue along the road until reaching the heart of the village where you will find a decorative street lamp commemorating Queen Victoria's coronation on June 28th 1838.

Branch right up the hill which loops into Sough Lane and over on your right is the cricket ground where you will find your car if you began your walk in Calver.

If you began your walk at Eyam, continue to the road junction with the B6001 turn right to the cross roads, then left to proceed along the A623 road to Stoney Middleton and Eyam which is the start/end of this walk.

The street lamp commemorating Queen Victoria's coronation